CONTENTS

With a Personal Introduction by
Martin Sheen

Words of WISDOM

A Collection of Inspirational Messages

VOLUME TWO

Fr W aun

Warren J. Rouse, OFM

Words of Wisdom
A Collection of Inspirational Messages
Volume Two
Warren J. Rouse, OFM

Cover images: Shutterstock.com
Cover and book design: Tau Publishing Design Department

Italics and boldface print in Scripture and quotations has been added by the author.

For information regarding permission, write to:
Tau Publishing, LLC
Attention: Permissions Dept.
4806 South 40th Street
Phoenix, AZ 85040

Paperback:
ISBN 978-1-61956-279-0
Hardcover:
ISBN: 978-1-61956-280-6

First Edition January 2015
10 9 8 7 6 5 4 3 2 1

Published and printed in the United States of America by Tau Publishing, LLC, an imprint of Vesuvius Press Incorporated.
For additional inspirational books visit us at TauPublishing.com

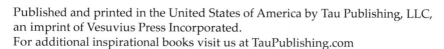

INTRODUCTION
BY MARTIN SHEEN

With his second book of inspirational meditations, Fr. Warren again offers his unique biblical insights with a disarming sense of humor. Page by page he leads us on another adventure of faith, hope and love. He is inviting us once again on a daring journey that unites the will of the Spirit with the work of the Flesh.

He is a senior Franciscan of the Province of Saint Barbara in California. He holds four postgraduate degrees and taught at San Luis Rey College and the University of San Diego. With the wisdom he has acquired throughout his career, he is uniquely qualified to share his knowledge and understanding with us.

Over a period of years he has published more than 300 articles and hundreds of book reviews for *The Way of Saint Francis* and other periodicals, nationally and internationally.

In his books I have found a joyful spirituality that inspires, refreshes and nourishes the soul. With this new edition Fr. Warren once again challenges our point of view, redirects our focus and invites us into the hidden nuggets of Scripture.

I have been blessed to know this remarkable man of faith. He, like so many other Franciscans that I have come to know, has enhanced my spiritual journey in ways that would be impossible to measure.

Welcome back!

—Martin Sheen
Actor

A LAKESIDE MEDITATION

MARK 1:29

Simon (Peter) is either an important person, or just outgoing. After Jesus finishes his homily in the Capernaum synagogue, Simon invites him and his disciples over for brunch after he first heals Simon's mother-in-law. (Mark 1:29) Nothing more than that. Except that during the meal the two men may be sizing each other up.

On another occasion Jesus is down by the lakeside, a popular place for both fishermen and vacationers. By this time it was not unusual that "the crowd was pressing in on him to hear the word of God." Jesus gets into Simon's boat and tells, not asks, him to "push a little off the shore" so the people could hear him better.

(Jesus takes people where they are. He doesn't say, "I will see you in church" or "I'm off duty now." We attend Sunday Mass: 50 or so minutes during which we feel that we're in contact with God. But what about the next 6 days? "The crowd was pressing in on him." They're eager, hopeful, clinging to His words. Are the Scriptures only for Sunday? And do we believe that Jesus can speak to us anywhere, and that there is no such thing as a "perfect, ideal place" for him to visit us?)

Simon (probably a bit miffed) and his crew are professionals, washing their nets and grumbling about their bad luck; they are more intent on their nets than on listening to Jesus who knows nothing about their trade. *(How often are we too preoccupied with "the cares of the world" to take the time simply to be with Jesus in our everyday life? Watch how often we say to ourselves or to others: "I'm too busy!")*

A sticky, testy scene follows: "When he had finished speaking, he said to Simon, 'Put out into the deep water and let down your nets for a catch.'" Surely this is a friendly reaching-out. But Jesus has inadvertently crossed a boundary: "Simon answered, 'Master, we have worked all night long but have caught nothing.'"

(Simon is saying: "You do your thing, but keep out of my work. What do YOU know about fishing?" And how often do we divorce ourselves from the Lord's inspirations in our workaday lives? Does He speak to us only at Mass on Sunday?)

And to emphasize his professionalism, Simon points out that his crew has "worked all night long and has already washed their nets." He deigns to explain to Jesus, perhaps with a touch of sarcasm, the elementary fact that real fishermen work at night, not during the daylight hours, for the best results. And obviously his men are not happy because they "have caught nothing."

(Through the centuries writers have talked about "the dark night of the soul," reminding us of St. Theresa of Avila or, in our day, Blessed Mother Theresa. Like them, we have times when prayer seems to be talking to ourselves, when we see disasters all around us, when we see thousands of children dying of starvation every day...and we ask: "Is there really a God? What's the use of a Church? What is faith? Do I have any?")

Simon unwittingly gives us the answer: "Yet if you say so, I will let down the nets." He's not convinced, or maybe he wants to prove a point, but he utters the words that can keep us going in our darkest moments: "if you say so," against all the odds. Sheer faith. Blaise Pascal righty said: "This faith in our hearts does not make us say, 'I know;' it makes us proclaim, 'I believe.'"

(Later on Jesus will give us the prayer: "Thy will be done on earth as it is in heaven." How easy it is to blithely utter this phrase, unthinking and parrot-like! But there will come a time—many times, perhaps—when we will virtually choke on these words.)

"So they signaled their partners in the other boat to come and help them. And they came and filled both boats, so that they began to sink. But when Simon Peter saw it, he fell down at Jesus' knees, saying, 'Go away from me, Lord, for I am a sinful man!'" *("Such is the fear of the one who discovers that God has entered into his inner life: this is a first act of faith in the divinity of Jesus, Yes, Jesus calls on sinners to save sinners."* (Catholic Community Bible)

Peter speaks for each of us: "Yet, if you say so..." "Thy will be done!"

A SACRED JOB DESCRIPTION

MATTHEW 9

St. Jerome wrote that the Scriptures are a personal letter written to each person. With that in mind, anyone who consistently reads the Scriptures will possibly come across a verse that seems to hold a special message.

Msgr. Ronald Knox wrote that the psalter, in particular, "has for each of us a private message. There are certain phrases which record landmarks in our own spiritual lives..." So he elaborates that when we come across these again, we can "trace a kind of secret code, a cipher by which God and the soul speak to one another."

A classic example of this is a Gospel verse (Matthew 9:10 TEV) that gave light to a searching Francis of Assisi: "Do not carry any gold, silver, or copper money in your pockets; do not carry a beggar's bag for the trip or an extra shirt or shoes or a walking stick." His biographer remembers Francis saying: This is what I want, this is what I seek, this is what I desire with all my heart." Franciscan poverty began!

For the future Pope Francis, another verse (Matthew 9:9) is what he pondered in his youth: "Jesus saw a man called Matthew sitting at the tax office, and he said to him: 'Follow me.'"

So deeply touched was Pope Francis that, at the age of 17, "following confession, his heart was touched by the descent of the mercy of God, who with tender love called him to the religious life, following the example of Saint Ignatius of Loyola."

In his further studies as a young man, he discovered the commentary of St. Bede the Venerable on Matthew's Gospel, and this verse in particular: "Our Lord summoned Matthew by speaking to him in words. By an invisible, interior impulse flooding his mind with the light of grace, he instructed him to walk in his footsteps."

"No doubt," William Barclay (*Daily Study Bible*) muses, "Matthew had listened on the outskirts of the crowd, and had felt his heart stir within him. Perhaps Matthew had wondered wistfully if even yet it was not too late to set sail and to seek a newer world, to leave his old life and his old shame and to begin again. So he found Jesus standing before him; he heard Jesus issue his challenge; and Matthew accepted that challenge and rose up and left all and followed him." Bishop N.T. Wright notes: "It was perhaps the first time for ages that someone had treated him as a human being instead of a piece of dirt." (Mark)

So it is not surprising that when he was ordained as an auxiliary bishop Francis chose for his coat of arms: *Miserando Atque Eligendo*—a short Latin phrase which means: "He (Jesus) saw him (Matthew) through eyes of mercy and chose him;" or: "Having mercy, he called him."

We know from the Pope's actions while archbishop in Argentina and in his early addresses in Rome, how he demonstrates a loving concern for those on the fringes of society—in particular, the poor, the destitute, the immigrants, those ignored by society. His words (July 8, 2013) concerning the plight of immigrants, especially those who drowned, are soul-wrenching:

"Who among us has wept for the immigrants, for the

dangers they faced and for the thousands who died at sea? *The globalization of indifference has taken from us the ability to weep...*" (Italics mine)

In choosing a penitential liturgy that day, the Pope said: "We ask forgiveness for our indifference toward so many brothers and sisters and for the ways in which well-being has anesthetized our hearts."

Mercy/compassion! A grace-filled choice! There's a reminder here: There are many, many moments in our seemingly uneventful lives when God's generous grace calls for a response. It may be a sudden, unexpected moment that will never come again. Succinctly the psalmist (95:7) urges: "O that today you would listen to his voice." *The Message* (Eugene Peterson) offers this contemporary translation: "Drop everything and listen, listen as he speaks."

And we join Pope Francis in prayer:

"Let us ask the Lord for the grace to weep over our indifference, to weep over the cruelty in the world, in ourselves, and even in those who anonymously make socio-economic decisions that open the way to tragedies like this."

Miserando Atque Eligendo: Having mercy, Jesus called him...and you.

A SURPRISE DETOUR
FOR SIMON

MARK 15:20

Jerusalem pilgrims look forward to the highlight of their visit: The Way of the Cross, conducted daily by Franciscans. They have been looking forward to following in the steps of Jesus and praying with great devotion.

Take it from me, folks, and I am an ancient friar in good standing:

It's hot, messy, noisy, with a lot of pushing, shouting and shoving. Shopkeepers on either side of the narrow street hawk their wares, inviting the people to detour into their shops or at least get out of the way. Forget about pious feelings!

And so it was in the time of Jesus–in stark contrast to the customary paintings of the tragic journey which show the Lord struggling along with soldiers leading the way and crowds orderly lining the street either to gawk or to commiserate. Awed silence seems to prevail.

Wrong! And the gospels bear this out. Mark, probably the earliest writer, merely states that "then they led him out to crucify him" (Mark. 15:20). There is nothing spectacular about this. The Romans see to public crucifixion as a lesson to the people lest they get any ideas about rebellion. Nothing too unusual here–in fact, as common as a freeway accident that invariably lures drivers to slow, look and then speed away.

Moreover, at this time of year Jerusalem is jam-packed with Jewish pilgrims from all over. They have other things on their minds especially shopping! Storekeepers have opened their doors (9:00A.M.) and don't like these "death parades" to block their entrances. They're impatient to keep things moving.

(Surely Jesus is thinking: "Doesn't anyone care? Doesn't anyone realize that I am doing this for them?" Sadly, there are merely a few people who *do* care. There is much here for meditation when we don't feel appreciated, when others do not recognize what we are doing for them, when we feel tossed aside because of old age or sickness, whenever we are no longer "productive" according to the world's standards.)

Enter now another figure: A gent from far away, Simon from Cyrene by name, has trudged to Jerusalem probably for the first and only time in his life, to celebrate the festival. Obviously he is decked out in his best clothes for this special occasion. But the dreaded Roman taps on his shoulder: he must assist in the carrying of the cross. So much for all his plans! "They compelled a passer-by, who was coming in from the country, to carry his cross; it was Simon of Cyrene, the father of Alexander and Rufus" (Mark 15:21). Imagine his disappointment and anger!

For his plans have been rudely interrupted indeed. He is being forced to perform a disgraceful action worthy only of a slave. He's a landowner! Why is he being picked on? He's just minding his own business.

How often we use that primitive phrase: "It's unfair!" When ugly things happen to us, when other people put us down, when tragedy strikes and all the while we're trying to be good Christians, Rabbi Abraham Heschel echoes our unspoken objection to this humiliation: "In the eyes of the world, I am an average man. But to my heart I am not an average man. To my heart I am of great moment. The challenge I face is how to actualize the quiet eminence of my being."

Perhaps Luke's gospel offers another, broader perspective for consideration, laying it at our own doorstep. He inserts an interesting variation: "as they led him away, they seized a man, Simon of Cyrene, who was coming from the country, and they laid the cross on him, and made him carry it behind Jesus" (Luke 23:26). Significantly, Luke alters Mark's words and meaning simply by adding, "and made him carry it behind Jesus."

Here indeed is the essence of discipleship: to follow Jesus. Simon has not heard the Lord say: "If anyone wants to come with me, he must forget himself, take up his cross every day, and follow me" (Luke 9:23). But he learns by doing.

As the story of Simon is open-ended, so is ours. Presumably Simon stays to the end of the day and hears the good news on Easter morning. Maybe Patriarch Bartholomew's 1996 Easter message reflects the sentiments and the unspoken message that Simon's finest hours bequeath to us:

"Remain to see the end. Each of you move and express yourself freely and personally. Flee along with Peter and John to the Tomb and you will believe in the Risen One. Stay with Mary close to the Tomb mourning and you will meet the Lord. Journey to Emmaus while reflecting on your problems; express your doubts; confess your hopelessness; and without recognizing Him you will find the Risen One at your side explaining to you your doubts."

ABOUT THOSE RELATIVES

MATTHEW 12:46

Two incidents in the Gospel of Matthew (Mark and Luke repeat them almost verbatim) always seems to have been, and are, controversial among Christians, including some Catholics. The first reference:

> "While he was still speaking to the crowds, his mother and his brothers were standing outside, wanting to speak to him. Someone told him, 'Look, your mother and your brothers are standing outside, wanting to speak to you.'"

> "But to the one who had told him this, Jesus replied, 'Who is my mother, and who are my brothers?' And pointing to his disciples, he said, 'Here are my mother and my brothers! For whoever does the will of my Father in heaven is my brother and sister and mother.'" (Matthew 12:46-50 (NRSV)

(Peterson's *The Message* has it: "Look closely. Obedience is thicker than blood. The person who obeys my heavenly Father's will is my brother and sister and mother.")

Then the second reference:

> "Isn't he the carpenter's son? Isn't Mary his mother, and aren't James, Joseph, Simon and Judas his

---

brothers? Aren't all his sisters living here? Where did he get all this? And so they rejected him." (Matthew 13:55)

(Peterson's paraphrase again: "He made a real hit, impressing everyone: 'We've known him since he was a kid: he's the carpenter's son. We know his mother, Mary. We know his brothers James and John, Simon and Judas. All his sisters live here. Who does he think he is?' They got their noses all out of joint.")

Apart from the traditional Catholic belief, not formally defined as a dogma, that Mary was a virgin before, during and after the birth of Jesus and remained so, there are two suggested explanations:

Some would read Matthew's statement (2:7) that "She gave birth to her first son" or, as others say, "firstborn," to indicate that the couple had other sons and daughters. Another view, a bit far-fetched—supposes that this was Joseph's second marriage and had children before marrying Mary. (Actually, neither of these hypotheses contradicts the Nicene Creed: "conceived by the power of the Holy Spirit.")

In this regard, the traditional Catholic position is nicely summarized: "...Matthew wishes to communicate two truths: (1) that Jesus is conceived virginally through the action of God...(2) that he is adopted by Joseph as his son, and so becomes part of the family of David. Jesus is thus both Son of God by conception and Son of David by adoption." (*The New Community Bible*)

And an early Church Father (Chromatius) writes: Not a few careless people insist on asking whether after the Lord's birth the holy mother Mary had relations with Joseph. But this is not admissible on the grounds of either faith or truth. Far be it indeed that after the sacrament of so great a mystery and after the birth of the sublime Lord, one should believe that the Virgin Mary was intimate with a man... It is not plausible that the Mary of the Gospel, a virgin bearing

God, who beheld God's glory not in a loud but was worthy of caring him in her virginal womb had relations with a man."

Finally, listen to what may seem to be a startling statement from St. Augustine: "Therefore it is greater for Mary to have been a disciple of Christ than the mother of Christ."

And Pope Benedict XVI concludes his encyclical, *Spe Salvi*, with these words directed to Mary:

> "No, at the foot of the Cross, on the strength of Jesus's own word, you became the mother of believers. In this faith, which even in the darkness of Holy Saturday bore the certitude of hope, you made your way towards Easter morning."

The joy of the Resurrection touched your heart and united you in a new way to the disciples, destined to become the family of Jesus through faith. In this way you were in the midst of the community of believers, who in the days following the Ascension prayed with one voice for the gift of the Holy Spirit (cf. Acts 1:14) and then received that gift on the day of Pentecost. The "Kingdom" of Jesus was not as might have been imagined. It began in that hour, and of this "Kingdom" there will be no end. Thus you remain in the midst of the disciples as their Mother, as the Mother of hope.

"Holy Mary, Mother of God, our Mother, teach us to believe, to hope, to love with you. Show us the way to his Kingdom! Star of the Sea, shine upon us and guide us on our way!"

AND HOW DO *YOU* PRAY?

Religion is not exempt from the search (sometimes frantic) for "new" forms of prayer. Only time separates the fads from the worthwhile. I tried, thanks to peer pressure, the still popular "shared prayer." It was a disaster.

First of all, even though it's not required, we sat or squatted on the floor in a circle—age, piety, and the body's plasticity making their own reluctant demands—not unlike boy scouts around the campfire. It was all very democratic.

Then, with eyes demurely cast down as befits grand humility, one inspired soul began to pray (or perhaps sigh) aloud. Heads nodded knowingly (at what, I could not fathom) and the occasional whispered "Amen" seemed to serve as celestial punctuation for truly banal and disjointed platitudes. It went on interminably.

Meanwhile, I was frantically searching for something in my public address to the Deity that would sound reasonably intelligent and perhaps edifying to these sainted souls. I toyed with the idea of speaking in tongues or even of being slain in the spirit. But that would appear ostentatious; instead I frantically conjured up something both vague and harmless, so bland that I have no recollection except for my relief when the séance was over.

Another faddish technique that I flunked miserably was "guided meditation" or something like that, where—back to the circle again—we closed our eyes while a guru had us "imagine you are sitting under a tree and an angel comes..." Every time I got trapped into one of these sessions. I shamelessly peeked. I felt like a voyeur, but I couldn't help it: I wanted to see if the other people were buying into this!

Perhaps many of us, if we rarely discuss our prayer life with others, would admit that we are usually more comfortable with "pre-made prayers." But we are reluctant to admit this because we've heard about "contemplative prayer" which seemingly occurs without the use of words. This is subtly communicated as some sort of "higher" or at least "preferred" prayer, leaving the rest of us as spiritual peasants (the Marthas rather than the Marys) stealthily carrying our cherished prayer books.

There are precedents and advantages to using "prepared prayers." Ruth Burrows explains that "it is a good thing to have something ready-made up our sleeve in case we find ourselves blank, something that will pull our thoughts to God and provide fodder for our minds." In the same vein, and to my relief, Cardinal Hume writes:

> "Each person is led differently. No two people pray in the same way, for instance, and what God reveals of himself to any individual is known to that person alone. That is one reason why we should listen to each other's experiences, for every person who takes the Christian life seriously has something important to say. It is often the unlearned and the deprived, as the world would judge, who have the clearest and deepest understanding of the things of God. (Cf. Matthew 11:25-26) It will, in fact, be so for those who are truly humble, whether learned or not."

There are times—and we wish these were not so few—when our conversation with the Lord is spontaneous and composed aids will simply get in the way. At other times we view prayer not as a privilege but as a duty: we honestly don't feel like praying. This "dark night of the soul" hits all of us without advance notice. Now we find prayer to be tedious, even distasteful and, worse, we seem simply to be babbling to ourselves. Here's where a cherished word or verse or prayer can "prime the pump," as it were. Or to put it another way: If you can't swim anymore, hold onto anything that's floating by!

Cardinal Hume is not reluctant to confess:

"As we grow older, we tend, I think, to be helped and inspired by fewer ideas than at an earlier period. Some 'thoughts' have become, over the years, familiar and trusted friends. They have served in the past; they are important now. We go back to them again and again for our own sakes."

"Lord, I know that I spend a certain amount of that morning hour of prayer daydreaming, problem-solving, and I'm not sure that I can cut that out. I'll try, but the important thing is, I'm not going to give that time to anybody else. So even though it may not unite me as much with you as it should, nobody else is going to get that time." (Cardinal Joseph Bernardin)

ANOTHER SIDE
TO THE STORY

LUKE 18

Several decades ago the terms "disposable" or "throwaway" generation were in vogue. And it still continues. Once we've had or experienced something—well, that's the end of that. Time to move on to the next novelty!

Often we bring the same attitude to the Scriptures: After we've read or heard a passage and understood the obvious meaning, a second reading strikes us as being simply repetitious–it's ho-hum time. We can almost borrow the phrase, "Been there! Done that!"

To help us explore the hidden riches of the Scripture, contemporary scholars encourage us to use our active imagination. This means to identify with a character or situation and prayerfully ponder: "What if...?" or "Suppose..." Using this technique, let's take a well known parable, whose meaning seems to be immediate, and explore it in more depth:

> He also told this parable to some who trusted in themselves that they were righteous and regarded others with contempt: "Two men went up to the temple to pray, one a Pharisee and the other a tax

collector. The Pharisee, standing by himself, was praying thus, 'God, I thank you that I am not like other people: thieves, rogues, adulterers, or even like this tax collector. I fast twice a week; I give a tenth of all my income.' But the tax collector, standing far off, would not even look up to heaven, but was beating his breast and saying, 'God, be merciful to me, a sinner!' I tell you, this man went down to his home justified rather than the other; for all who exalt themselves will be humbled, but all who humble themselves will be exalted." (Luke 18:9-14)

So far we have the good guy/bad guy syndrome as the *personae dramatis*. Pharisees are basically learned and pious lay persons dedicated to a scrupulous observance of the Law and—this is where they err—a multitude (over 600!) of non-Scriptural traditions. Some tend to be rigid nitpickers.

Continuing on with this parable, the "tax collector" definitely needs no introduction. The unspoken job description says it all: cheater. As far as his neighbors are concerned he has absolutely no redeeming qualities. He's a traitor to his own. Time for the "what if" possibilities:

Suppose that the Pharisee has been busy all morning: first, he does his stint with Meals on Wheels; then he stops to visit some sick people; he quietly gives alms to a beggar; he helps a crippled person up the stairs and into the Temple. On the other hand, suppose the tax collector has not been idle. This very morning he has evicted two families from their homes because they're behind in their rent; he closes down a shop that hasn't turned in its sales tax on time; he confiscates a street vendor's license; he rudely scolds a beggar and shoves him aside. At this point in the scenario (Who's to say that it is not a possibility?) the Pharisee is the good guy and the tax collector is the bad.

But the picture quickly changes: "The Pharisee, standing by himself, was praying thus, 'God, I thank you that I am not like other people: thieves, rogues, adulterers, or even like this tax collector. I fast twice a week; I give a tenth of all my income.'" Note the fact that he is "standing by himself," a solid clue that he is placing himself above and separate from The Great Unwashed. He's in the first pew! Note also that he, rather than God, is the center of pious attention. "But the tax collector stood at a distance and would not even raise his face to heaven, but beat on his breast and said, 'God, have pity on me, a sinner.'"

The story is open-ended (that's the genius of parables) for our benefit: Does the Pharisee eventually acquire the gift of honesty (humility) in his life? And the tax collector: he indeed goes home justified *at this moment*, but does he then give up his notorious ways? Something to think about!

For us individually, we need to study well known passages such as this one and place ourselves within them. New meanings for the same words will come to us. St. Ephraem exhorts us:

> *"Lord, who can grasp all the wealth in just one of your words? What we understand is much less than what we leave behind, like thirsty people who drink from a fountain. For your word, Lord, has many shades of meaning just as those who study it have many different points of view. The Lord has colored his words with many hues so that each person who studies it can see in it what he loves. He has hidden many treasures in his word so that each of us is enriched as we meditate on it."*

DRESS YOUR BEST

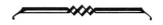

PSALM 9:22

The trouble is…so often we read or hear certain phrases repeatedly and therefore (understandably) glide over their meaning. That's why, in Bible study, one of the best methods is simply to compare several translations.

Here's an example from Psalm 29:2: the sacred writer is encouraging us to praise the Lord *"in splendore sancto"*— literally, "in holy splendor." While we complacently nod in agreement with this, exactly what does "in holy splendor" mean for us?? Time to check out some quite respectable and scholarly translations. (Bear with me: there's going to be a point to this!)

The New Jerusalem Bible: "In the splendor of holiness." That's not helpful. The *Christian Community Bible* has an almost incomprehensible "in great liturgy." The Jewish *Tanakah*) indicates a place: "In his holy court." *The New American Bible* (used at Mass) prefers "the Lord's holy splendor," equally vague! The favored *New Revised Standard Version* is content with "in holy splendor."

If you've followed along this far, consider that several other translations have a different slant. "In holy splendor" becomes "in holy attire" for the *Revised English Version*, and *Today's English Version* echoes this with "in garments of worship." But I think that Eugene Peterson's paraphrase version (*The Message*) really captures the meaning and the spirit of "in holy splendor" with the remarkable, "Stand at attention! Dress your best to honor him."

Following Peterson, let's talk about "church and dress" and what the implications are. I remember reading a 1914 (!) haberdashery ad in a church bulletin: "If you don't think that clothes make the man, try walking down the street without any," which I thought was quite risqué for those days! (As a boy I also remember going to Sunday Mass and having several classmates disparage me for not being as well dressed as they were. That hurt because all I had was a sweat shirt and jeans. We were poor.)

For me, Peterson's translation best reflects the scriptural translation: "Dress your best to honor him." In this age of casualness which belittles or ignores and often masks plain old laziness, have we sometimes lost a sense of civility even in our worship services?

Oh, yes, some will excuse their indifference with the response that "Jesus is my buddy" or with that ghastly "I've got to be me," or the clincher, "I'm demonstrating my fundamental option for the poor," thus absolving them of courtesy and respect toward their neighbor and, indeed, toward God.

It's just here Peterson has a telling observation that indirectly affects our deportment and, yes, our clothing, at times of public worship. He writes:

"We (Americans) would rather pray by exploring our own deep spiritual capacities, with God as background music. We would rather pray by meditating on some sublime truth, without bothering with the tedium and complexity of the scriptures. We would rather pray by having God all to ourselves, insulated from the irritating presence of other people, and savor (but only a little) a smug sense of superiority to the common herd..."

If clothes DO make the man, what we wear—and maybe this is a truism—DOES influence our behavior. For years, institutions from schools to roller-skating rinks have experienced the practical value of dress codes.

This leads us to a self-examination of our approach to public worship (liturgy). In a word, what are our values here? Do we feel it important to "dress up" to some extent when we attend Mass? I am not talking about expensive clothing selected and designed to "show off" one's financial status. There simply needs to be attire *appropriate to the occasion*— below tuxedos and above men's walking shorts *cum* tennis shoes or women's sometimes scanty attire. (Believe me, as a priest distributing communion, I've seen it all!)

Even that pagan writer, Cicero, says: "He who takes reverence from friendship, takes away its brightest jewel." Our dress, our posture at Mass have a direct bearing on a sense of holiness, of awe, so sadly missing today. Rabbi Heschel reminds us: "A return to reverence is the first prerequisite for a revival of wisdom."

Moses was instructed: "Remove your sandals from your feet. You're standing on holy ground." At every Eucharist we are standing on holy ground. Shouldn't we dress properly for the occasion? "Dress your best to honor him!"

ELIJAH ON THE RUN

I KINGS 18-19

The first Book of Kings (has a great story about the trials and tribulations of the prophet Elijah. Similar to most of the prophets, Elijah is not a happy camper.

The incident happens during a drought. The reigning king is Ahab (a rather wishy-washy character); and his notorious queen—Jezebel—who basically wears the royal pants in the family). The Lord tells Elijah, their persistent nemesis, to meet with the king. Both parties are ambivalent: there is no love lost between them over the widespread paganism championed by Jezebel.

"Is it you, you troubler of Israel?" Ahab asks. No apology, but a blunt charge. "I have not troubled Israel; but you have, and your father's house, because you have forsaken the commandment of the Lord and followed the Baals."

After a row which the Lord and Elijah win, the prophet goes on a roll, destroying the pagan temples and slaughtering the priests. During their pillow talk, Ahab reluctantly tells the queen what Elijah has done. Absolutely furious, Jezebel sends this message to the prophet: "So may the gods do to me and more also, if I do not make your life like the life of one of them by this time tomorrow." In plain English: "You're dead meat."

Elijah's reaction was simple: "Then he was afraid. He got up and fled for his life." Leaving his personal servant behind him he fled a day's journey out of town. This was a low time in his life and he felt like giving up. While he sat under a tree he prayed bluntly: "It is enough; now, O Lord, take away my life for I am no better than my ancestors."

Exhausted, he fell asleep—but not for long: "Suddenly an angel touched him," provided some food and told the prophet to hit the road again. But Elijah went back to sleep. Again the angel prodded him, fed him and "then he went in the strength of that food forty days and forty nights to Horeb the mount of God. At that place he came to a cave, and spent the night there."

That's an interesting detail because in ancient times a cave symbolized depression, loneliness, and even death. Clearly Elijah has given up and opts for Sheol (the shadowy after-life also known as the Land of Silence.)

But the Lord calls him out of the cave, "for the Lord is about to pass by." Sure enough, three traditional epiphanies (exclusive signs of God's presence) come about: a strong wind, an earthquake, and a fire. But God is not in these; What follows is "a sound of sheer silence" (NRSV) or "a tiny whispering sound (NAB)."

This simple verse invites us to pause for personal reflection about the role and importance of silence in our prayer times.

Your own experience should demonstrate that it is practically useless to switch immediately from a beehive of mental activities to the concentration of prayer. It just doesn't work! There must be a sort of "de-briefing" time to clear the mind from this all-important graced moment. (The same is true for liturgical prayer, especially the Eucharist. Rushing into Mass at the very last moment is not conducive to an attentive listening of the Word.)

Silence needs to be an essential element in our personal prayer. Frankly, we are more comfortable with reciting memorized prayers or instructing the Lord how to run the universe. Certainly, and especially when we are tired, ready-made prayers can help greatly. But silence can be and should be prayer, also: just being in the presence of the Lord. Nothing more.

Metropolitan Anthony Bloom speaks of silence:

"This we can do, and we must be able to do it. But it requires systematic, intelligent training, in exactly the same way as we train to do other things. Learn to master time, and you will be able, whatever you do, whatever the stress, in the storm, in tragedy, or simply in the confusion in which we continuously live—to be still, immobile in the present, face to face with the Lord, in silence or in words."

Thomas Merton writes: "Solitude is not found so much by looking outside the boundaries of your dwelling as by staying within them." Solemn, stern words! But cheer up! He is one of us: "There is nothing to live for but God, and I am still full of the orchestras that drown His voice." And John Calvin confesses:

"Surely, just as waters boil up from a vast, full spring, so does an immense crowd of gods flow forth from the human mind...Man's nature, so to speak, is a perpetual factory of idols!"

Don't be discouraged—we're in good company!

EXCUSES, EXCUSES!

LUKE 9

Sometimes, but not often, prayer seems joyous and we say with Peter on the mount of Transfiguration: "It is good for us to be here." (Luke 9:8) Maybe Peterson's translation is more accurate: "He blurted this out without thinking!"

We've all had these moment, reckless as they may be, of promising the Lord everything. It's happened to all of us. It's not a new phenomenon. There are three incidents in Luke's gospel which are instructive.

The <u>first</u> is the person who's all fired up in a fit of pious enthusiasm. "As they were going along the road, someone said to him, 'I will follow you wherever you go.'" On the positive side the nameless, unthinking man places no reservations or conditions on his spontaneous intention: the path is clear and inviting! But, negatively, he hasn't thought things through. Jesus recognizes this: And Jesus is curt. Eugene Peterson (*The Message*) paraphrases the response nicely: "Are you ready to rough it? We're not staying in the best inns, you know."

In our own lives it is easy—when everything's going well—to make all sorts of unreflective promises to the Lord. But "first fervors" are notoriously transitory; and when the balloon bursts, what is left? Paraphrasing the marriage vows, we declare our loyalty to the Lord "in good times and in bad, in sickness and in health." When the rough times come, however, we tend to fall back into the rut of mediocrity, of going through the motions of prayer and service. At any rate, we will never know what decision the man in the Gospel makes.

The second instance is surprisingly different because it is the Lord who takes the initiative and, for whatever reason, is impressed with the man: "To another he said, 'Follow me.'" Again this man quickly agrees but with a condition: "Certainly, but excuse me for a couple of days. I have to make arrangements for my father's funeral." (Peterson)

The Lord's curious reply, at face value, seems both cold and callous: "Let the dead bury their own dead; but as for you, go and proclaim the kingdom of God." ("First things first. Your business is life, not death. And life is urgent: Announce God's kingdom." – Peterson)

Over the centuries scholars have argued the case both ways: is it literal or symbolic? St. Basil the Great doesn't mince words: "A person who wishes to become the Lord's disciple must repudiate a human obligation, however honorable it may appear, if it slows us ever so slightly in giving the wholehearted obedience we owe to God." For Basil—case closed!

The Christian Community Bible reflects a more understandable and compassionate tradition: "Most probably it means that he wanted to look after his aging father up to the time of his burial," or at least "(Jesus) is not giving a directive to be applied in all cases." In other words, He is addressing only one man on one specific occasion.

The infamous bottom line: Jesus is asking for unreserved dedication *according to each person's grace*. We all experience situations that keep us necessarily occupied with "secular" concerns. But even in the midst of these we can be united with the Lord. How? St. Augustine replies: "I can give you a tip that will enable you to praise God throughout the day, if you want to. Whatever you have to do, do it well, and you have praised God."

The <u>third</u> "first fervor" attack is when another person says, "I will follow you, Lord; but let me first say farewell to those at my home." (Peterson: "But first excuse me while I get things straightened out at home.")

We're all tempted to procrastinate! Even admirable St. Francis! In his final words (Testament) he recalls: "And afterwards I delayed a little and left the world." We're in good company here! In a famous poem Francis Thompson mirrors our universal predicament, our fear of risk-taking:

I fled Him, down the nights and down the days;
    I fled Him, down the arches of the years;
I fled Him down the labyrinthine ways
    Of my own mind; and in the midst of tears
I hid from Him, and under running laughter.

"No one," Jesus explains, "who puts a hand to the plow and looks back is fit for the kingdom of God." In contemporary language: "No procrastination. No backward looks. You can't put God's kingdom off until tomorrow. Seize the day."

Perhaps Blessed Junípero Serra in a few words captures the message: "Always go forward—never turn back!"

FAMILIARITY BREEDS FORGETFULNESS

Ah, yes—in days gone by we attended Mass. Today, if you're really "with it," we "do Eucharist." That's the "in" expression, at least until someone comes up with another hokey idea! Regardless of this as well as the mandated liturgical changes that come dribbling forth with precious little reason or sensitivity, there will always be a problem with public worship.

Indeed, years ago the famed anthropologist, Margaret Meade, pointed out a situation peculiar to Catholics at worship: repetition is likely to produce boredom and distraction because we hear and pray the same words so often. (Be honest now—haven't you drifted off into fantasy land when a well known Scripture passage is read? And don't we often "say" the prayers mechanically without thinking about them?)

The Our Father is a good example. Toward its end is "and lead us not into temptation." But what do these simple and seemingly obvious words really mean? First of all, we somehow associated temptation with being sinful. How often in going to Confession (Sorry—now it's "Reconciliation!") a penitent would wind the whole thing up—to cover all bases, as it were—by saying that he/she has been tempted. Frankly, my unspoken response is: "So what else is new?" Temptation is neutral: it's neither good nor bad and it is more often than not spontaneous: it just happens. It's what we do about it, as Jimmy Carter so memorably recounted.

Secondly, and of much more importance, is the fact that taken at face value "and lead us not into temptation" almost implies blasphemy! The implication, again at face value, is that God can go against his goodness and love and somehow be able to lure and entrap us! Sort of a "gotcha!" situation.

Since that cannot be the case, what does the phrase mean? Of all the translations in English, I find the one that makes the most sense is: "Keep us safe from ourselves." Granted that it is a paraphrase rather than a literal rendition of the Greek, it seems to capture what Jesus really meant in giving us this prayer. "Keep watch," he says in the Garden, "and pray that you will not fall into temptation. The spirit is willing, but the flesh is weak" (Matthew 26:41).

Later on, St. Paul gives this encouragement: "Every test that you have experienced is the kind that normally comes to people. But God keeps his promise, and he will not allow you to be tested beyond your power to remain firm; at the time you are put to the test, he will give you the strength to endure it, and so provide you with a way out" (2 Corinthians 10:13 TEV).

The Lord's prayer, in paraphrase, goes on: "Keep us safe from ourselves and from the Devil." For many folks the mention of "Devil" is quaint at best, silly at worst. We so-called "postmoderns" have long abandoned the image of the horns, tail and pitchfork. In our sophistication we have risen above such "nonsense."

In that timeless book, *The Screwtape Letters*, C.S. Lewis has a senior devil instructing a junior colleague: "The fact that 'devils' are predominantly *comic* figures in the modern imagination will help you. If any faint suspicion of your existence begins to arise...suggest to him a picture of something in red tights, and persuade him [the one being tempted] that since he cannot believe in that (it is an old textbook method of confusing them) he therefore cannot believe in you."

Whether we choose to pray for deliverance from evil or from the Devil, the petition, and our personal experience, recognizes that there is indeed disorder within us. St. Paul expressed this quite dramatically in recalling some mysterious ailment (which Scripture scholars have never figured out): "Three times I prayed to the Lord about this and asked him to take it away. But his answer was: 'My grace is all you need, for my power is greatest when you are weak'" (2 Corinthians 12:9 TEV).

Later, in his commentary on the Our Father, St. Augustine ponders the words, "Deliver us from evil":

"We are reminding ourselves to reflect on the fact that we do not yet enjoy the state of blessedness in which we shall suffer no evil. This is the final petition contained in the Lord's Prayer, and it has a wide application. In this petition the Christian can utter his cries of sorrow, in it he can shed his tears, and through it he can begin, continue and conclude his prayer, whatever the distress in which he finds himself. Yes," he concludes, "it was very appropriate that all these truths should be entrusted to us to remember in these very words."

In his own simple way, St. Francis cuts to the quick and offers us a quite succinct but easily remembered way of praying the last two petitions of the prayer:

And lead us not into temptation:
    hidden or obvious,
    sudden or persistent.

But deliver us from evil:
    past,
    present,
    and to come.

FISHING FOR MONEY

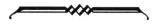

MATTHEW 17:24

When the Letter to the Hebrews says that Jesus "had to become like his brothers and sisters in every way," (Hebrews 2:17), that includes taxes! And there are several of them!

First, there is the civil Roman tax and Jesus has no problem with this: "Well, then, pay to the Emperor what belongs to the Emperor, and pay to God what belongs to God (Matthew 22:21)." But the squabble—recorded only in Matthew's Gospel—has to do with the temple tax.

Apparently in Jesus' time the rule is that every male Jew 19-20 years of age or older is required to pay a half-shekel annually for the maintenance of the temple service. This doesn't sound like much, but actually it is the equivalent of 2 days' pay for the average worker. Refusal to pay theoretically means that the delinquent person no longer wants to be a part of the religious community.

Now the controversy. Jesus has come back to his second home, Capernaum, and the local religious leaders approach not Jesus but Peter: "Does your teacher not pay the temple tax" (Matthew 17:24)? Actually the more precise translation is: "Your teacher pays the temple tax, doesn't he?" Peter assures them that Jesus does (or at least he thinks he pays the tax!) It's just here that Jesus takes the opportunity to explain that he is actually tax-exempt:

"What do you think, Simon? From whom do kings of the earth take toll or tribute? From their children or from others?' When Peter said, 'From others,' Jesus said to him, 'Then the children are free'" (17:-26-27). To put it another way: God is his father, his king, and Jesus is his son" Kings don't tax their own sons!

That is a perfectly valid but legalistic viewpoint. Jesus can, if he wishes, assert his right not to conform. But notice that he waives his prerogative: "However, so that we do not give offense to them..." (17:27). What a splendid attitude and model for us!

How often do we insistently act on a perfectly legitimate right even though we don't have to? To "give in," according to our contemporary narcissistic society, is a sign of weakness. Jesus isn't reluctant to go the extra mile if a greater good— that of someone else—can be achieved. But no—"I have a right to" seems almost to be the first words that a baby learns! Selfishness and egotism begin early in life and grow and grow.

St. Paul has the same attitude as Jesus over the issue of food sacrificed to idols. Since idols do not exist, why not eat that food? But he says (I Corinthians 8:9): "Be careful not to let your freedom of action make those who are weak in the faith fall into sin," or in this instance be punished for not paying the tax.

Matthew scholar Douglas Hare remarks that our Christian freedom "is subject to restriction for the sake of the brothers and sisters in the church as well as of those outside...Jesus' followers are advised not to give unnecessary offense on secondary issues where principle is not involved and compromise is possible."

Consider several examples: You have the right of way at a signed intersection; perhaps the driver on your left inches out before you. Is this a time for horn-honking and gestures? Or you're going through a swinging door—you have a right to, but do you ever look back to see if someone's behind you, perhaps with bags of groceries? Again: You have a perfect right to drink alcoholic beverages—but if you're with a recovering alcoholic might it not be more considerate to abstain?

Small instances, but most of life is made up of small things. Must individual rights always supersede graciousness? Jesus reminds us in this story that "rights" are relative to kindness and sensitivity.

Back to religious taxes. Matthew relates a startling, quite out-of-character instruction that Jesus gives to Peter: "Go to the sea and cast a hook; take the first fish that comes up; and when you open its mouth, you will find a coin; take that and give it to them for you and me."

A disturbing direction indeed! This has rightly puzzled many because it is so unlike Jesus. He never works miracles for his own gratification and he certainly never wants to be seen as some sort of magician. A number of possible, sometimes wild, explanations have been brought forth over the centuries, but perhaps William Barclay (*Daily Study Bible*) offers the more sensible explanation:

"Let us remember again the Jewish love of dramatic vividness. Undoubtedly what happened was this. Jesus said to Peter: 'Yes, Peter. You're right. We, too, must pay our just and lawful debts. Well, you know how to do it. Back you go to the fishing for a day. You'll get plenty of money in the fishes' mouths to pay our dues! A day at the fishing will soon produce all we need!'"

How does that affect your own prayer life?

GIVE ME A BREAK!

LUKE 7-10

Sometimes—maybe often—we hear or read a Gospel parable that doesn't make sense to us. And even if we do understand the story, it is likely to remain a puzzle that's difficult to apply in our own lives. Here's a classic translation (*The Message*):

> "Suppose one of you has a servant who comes in from plowing the field or tending the sheep. Would you take his coat, set the table, and say, 'Sit down and eat'? Wouldn't you be more likely to say, 'Prepare dinner; change your clothes and wait table for me until I've finished my coffee; then go to the kitchen and have your supper'?"

> "Does the servant get special thanks for doing what's expected of him? It's the same with you. When you've done everything expected of you, be matter-of-fact and say, 'The work is done. What we were told to do, we did.'"

Because our first reaction is that the boss-man (you) is heartless, even cruel, Jesus tells the story to instruct us about our own lives...specifically, about our prayer lives.

First, there are occasions when we feel that our Lord

isn't even listening to us. Do you remember (Luke 8:22-25) the time when the apostles thought they were drowning in a storm? And Jesus was fast asleep—the ultimate insult! As Metropolitan Anthony Bloom paraphrases their words to Jesus: "If you can do nothing, at least don't sleep. If you can do nothing better, then at least die in anguish with us."

Second, there are times when we feel that praying is simply talking to ourselves, simply babbling or, at best, instructing an absent God on how to run the world in general and our desires in particular. And nothing, absolutely nothing happens. What a waste of time! What we don't gasp is what many a spiritual writer has said: "The language of God is silence." And that's hard to take.

And third, to return to the original parable: Recall just two instances: Sr. Theresa, the great Carmelite reformer, wrote that she had absolutely no experience of God for 17 years. And in recent times, to the shock of many, Mother Teresa writes in her autobiography the absence of God in her years of working with the poor.

That's all very well and we readily admire, from a distance, the great, heroic saints of the past with all their fastings, fights with the devil and so on. But that's not us and not our lives.

Even in the spiritual realm we are products of our own culture. It is a firm belief that we should be rewarded for our labors, be it a just wage, merits and benefits. And this, we unconsciously believe, should hold for the spiritual life.

We pray (with little success but consistently), we volunteer in our parishes and other organizations to help the poor, we make sacrifices for strangers; in short, we try to live a good life for God. But where are the rewards, the perks, for our labors?

Martin Luther offer this thought about our ho-hum lives:

"God does not consider how little, or how great

the works are, but God looks on the heart, which performs in faith and obedience to God the demands of its calling...God pays no heed to the insignificance of the work being done, but looks at the heart which is serving him in the work; and this is true of such mundane tasks as washing the dishes or milking the cows."

Back to the parable: "Does the servant get special thanks for doing what's expected of him? It's the same with you. When you've done everything expected of you, be matter-of-fact and say, 'The work is done. What we were told to do, we did.'" And in faith we believe:

There is nothing in all creation that will ever be able to separate us from the love of God, which is ours through Christ our Lord. (Luke 8:39)

GO TO - WHERE?

So what—in Old Testament times—happens when a person dies? Certainly there was the common belief (and even today) that life ends with death and people—good or bad, it simply makes no difference—are consigned to a place called Sheol—a land of shadows and silence.

Through the centuries there have been various translations of this strange word. Literally, Sheol in Hebrew means "to be extinguished;" variant translations will call it the netherworld, the underworld, hades, the grave or, late in Christian times, hell.

The primary concept of Sheol is simply the place where all people, both the just and the wicked, end up. As Eeerdman's *Dictionary of the Bible* states: "The concept of an afterlife was relatively undeveloped in Israel's early period." There is no concept of a personal resurrection.

Even now Jewish people are frankly not preoccupied about "life after death." A modern Jewish writer, Roy Rosenberg (*The Concise Guide to Judaism*), sums it up: "What might legitimately be said is that Jews in general, the Orthodox as well as the non-Orthodox, do not stress a belief in the survival of the soul as a major aspect of Jewish commitment." Unlike Christians, "there are relatively few

Jews of any persuasion who would say that they participate in religious life because they hope for a heavenly reward."

There is abundant confirmation of this especially in the Old Testament, For example:

"What mortal can live and not see death? Who can escape the power of Sheol?" (Psalm 89:49)

"For who among the dead remembers you? Who praises you in Sheol?" (6:5)

While there is a definite finality described here, there are other verses which express an expanded thought not exclusively reserved to physical death:

"But God will redeem my life, will take me from the power of Sheol."(55:16)

"I was caught by the cords of death; the snares of Sheol had seized me; I felt agony and dread." (116:3)

Renowned biblical scholar Roland Murphy explains what is happening here. He says that Sheol "stands for things that are quite real: sickness, opposition, personal unhappiness and failure, enemies. In other words, all the obstacles one faces in daily life–these are manifestations of Sheol; one is in the 'hand' or power of Sheol." (Psalm 89:49) Murphy leans toward the translation of Sheol as "non-life."

"To the extent that we experience non-life, to that extent we are in Sheol. This is a profound insight into reality: **Death exercises a dominion over us long before we die. We may not trivialize this in terms of the aging process about which we can do nothing.** No, Sheol stands for whatever beleaguers us, overwhelms us.

St. Ambrose in one of his homilies sets the right tone for Christians:

"Death then must already be active in us if life too is

to be active..." And so the apostle [Paul] teaches us that we must embrace Christ's death while we are still alive in this world... Contemplating the many Sheols we experience in our lives, he says that "death in this sense is a pilgrimage, a lifetime's pilgrimage which none must shrink...from mortality to immortality, from anxiety to unruffled calm."

"For you are with me;
your rod and your staff–
they comfort me." (23:4)

A final thought that Murphy adds: As Christians we are accustomed to minimize this world's trials and setbacks with the thought that heaven is the only worthwhile end to be considered. But he reminds us that—and this is worth remembering—the Jews "lived with God in the present, and so must we even if we have a belief in a future life." In a nutshell:

"It is the present that decides the future."

GO WITH THE WINNER

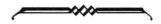

REVELATION 2FF

Chances are that the least understood book in the Bible is *Revelation* or, as it's also described in some circles, *Apocalypse*. First, it's written in an apocalyptic style which, in a word, deals with a somewhat bizarre future. Second, it seems to have been written in a code which only contemporaries really understood.

Still, this book is especially popular with preachers of doom and scripture students trying to figure out what all the numbers mean. The result is that *Revelation*, still flamboyantly vague, gives license to all sorts of "far out" interpretations.

But even for us ordinary persons of faith, there is much—positive and negative—that can be gleaned for our spiritual lives. The author's address to the seven churches of the day can actually give us encouragement.

The Church of Ephesus flunks: "But I have this against you, that you have abandoned the love you had at first." (*And isn't that the danger for us? What has happened to our first enthusiasm for our prayer life?*)

Smyrna's Church fares better, but with a caution: "Be faithful until death" because hard times are on their way.

(*It's a reminder to us to be realistic about our spiritual life—it's not always a sweet and comforting path.*)

Then there's **Pergamum**: "But I have this against you, that you have abandoned the love you had at first." (*How timely—as we see "Drop-outs" maybe in our own families, who have abandoned the universal and local churches because of uncovered sinfulness. As if Jesus had promised perfection!*)

The Church in **Thyatira** has a puzzling criticism: "You tolerate that woman Jezebel, who calls herself a prophet and is teaching and beguiling my servants..." (*Note the evangelical preachers who entice people with the absolute certainty of heaven, thus creating factions or at least doubts in the worshipping community.*)

Sardis gets a devastating condemnation: "I know your works; you have the name of being alive, but you are dead." (*Perhaps this is directed to a parish always inward, that only takes care of itself with no regard for the rest of the Church. I remember as a "freshman" pastor how I resented those special collections for many different needs! "We need the money here!"*)

Now to the **Church of Philadelphia**: "I know that you have but little power, and yet you have kept my word and have not denied my name." And a good word: "I am coming soon, hold fast to what you have, so that no one can seize your crown." (*In this catalog of churches, here is where we want to belong—with the folks of the ancient city of Philadelphia! With them, we try to be devoted lovers of God in Jesus Christ.*)

But wait! Here is a healthy warning aimed at the **Church of Laodicea** that should scare us: "I know your works; you are neither cold nor hot. I wish that you were either cold or hot. So, because you are lukewarm, and neither cold nor hot, I am about to spit you out of my mouth." (*Yes, it is only too easy for us to become backsliders, as it were. We begin to take God and his concerns (including his people) for granted. "Let others take care of the poor, the sick, the imprisoned."*)

No matter how messy the Church of Laodicea may be, the Lord says to it and to us in our own messiness this very day:

> "Be in earnest, then, and turn from your sins. Listen! I stand at the door and knock; if anyone hears my voice and opens the door, I will come into his house and eat with him, and he will eat with me." (3:18)

But, you still object, I always seem to fall short of my own expectations. It's all very discouraging. Just here St. Bernard of Clairvaux offers a surprising suggestion, a remedy in such dark times:

> "My advice to you, friends, is to turn aside from troubled and anxious reflection on your own progress...Sorrow for sin is, indeed, a necessary thing, but it should not prevail all the time."

> **"It is necessary, rather, that happier recollections of the divine bounty should counterbalance it, lest the heart should become hardened through too much sadness and so perish through despair."**

GOOD OL' ZEKE

LUKE 19

There are times—rare, to be sure—when being a former Greek and Latin teacher comes in handy. The benefit is that the story of Zaccaheus (recorded only in St. Luke's Gospel, chapter 19) may actually have a different twist to it.

"He entered Jericho and was passing through it. A man was there named Zacchaeus; he was a chief tax collector (a CEO) and was rich." You couldn't ask for anything worse—tax collectors are frequently lumped together in the gospels; they may be rich but they're still "trailer trash."

"He was trying to see who Jesus was, but on account of the crowd he could not, because he was short in stature." As often is the case, he's a pushy sort of fellow but he knows what he wants: to see this Jesus–simply as an observer with no intention of becoming involved.

"So he ran ahead and climbed a sycamore tree to see him, because he was going to pass that way." Zacchaeus doesn't stroll, or stand and gawk–even suited up in his office best he climbs up a tree. In other words, he knows what he wants and "goes for it." He is universally hated so he cares less about the jokes and jibes of the onlookers. Dignity and appearances give way to determination. (And what price are we willing to pay, as it were, to find Jesus... despite the cultural obstacles around us?)

"When Jesus came to the place, he looked up and said to him, 'Zacchaeus, hurry and come down...'" How does Jesus know this fellow's name? Is Zacchaeus *that* notorious in town? Does Jesus hear people in the crowd jeering and pointing their finger at the man perched in the tree? No matter: what is touching is that Jesus calls him by name. He recognize him as a person–and that probably hasn't happened very often, given Z's despicable occupation.

"...for I must stay at your house today. So he hurried down and was happy to welcome him." Notice the unexpected self-invitation: Jesus tells him to "hurry" and Zaccahaeus "hurried down." Spiritual writers often emphasize the importance of those unexpected, graced moments in our daily lives that will never come again—reminiscent of that film, *The Dead Poets' Society* and the theme: "Carpe diem!– Seize the day!"

"All who saw it began to grumble and said, 'He has gone to be the guest of one who is a sinner.'" Remember the book title, *When Bad Things Happen to Good People?* We can usually figure that out. The crowd's problem is the opposite: they, and we, go bananas "when good things happen to bad people!" That's the situation here.

"Zacchaeus stood there and said to the Lord, 'Look, half of my possessions, Lord, I will give to the poor; and if I have defrauded anyone of anything, I will pay back four times as much.'" Now it's precisely at this point that Greek and Latin are important because most of the contemporary translations are not completely accurate. In both languages *the present tense is used, not the future!* And this changes the meaning dramatically. The text should read, as Peterson (*The Message*) correctly captures it: "Master, I give away half my income to the poor–and if I'm caught cheating, I pay four times the damage." Do you see the impact of this?

First, in this regard Zacchaeus is not called to repent

because he may have nothing to repent for! Second, the crowd has automatically and falsely categorized him as a sinner. They have given him a label and they treat him accordingly without any knowledge of his intrinsic goodness and generosity. (And how often do we label people negatively because of our ignorance, not unlike one of the early Fathers of the Church, Cyril of Alexandria, who bluntly told his congregation: "Zacchaeus was leader of the tax collectors, a man entirely abandoned to greed, whose only goal was the increase of his gains." (So much for charity...)

"Then Jesus said to him, 'Today salvation has come to this house, because he too is a son of Abraham.'" Jesus is not about to back off. He almost sarcastically reminds "the good people" that Zacchaeus is one of theirs by blood and religion. In their eyes he may be a black sheep–but he's still a sheep! And Jesus does not tell him to change jobs!

But "salvation has come to this house"–words directed to us this very day. Over and over we are invited to conversion by "this man who eats with sinners" (Augustine).

Zacchaeus may well be a patron saint for our time.

HELP WANTED

MATTHEW 15:21-28

A contemporary American slogan: "If at first you don't succeed–forget it!" This may well apply to the world of business, but our own and the lives of uncountable others deny its validity.

There's a marvelous but homey example of persistence in Matthew's gospel. Jesus has crossed the borders into gentile territory despite his operating principle that his mission is only and exclusively to the Jewish people. And moreover, in the culture of his time, women are definitely second class. When Jesus meets (a) a pagan who is (b) a woman, Timothy Radcliffe, O.P., writes this overview:

"This incident is part of a slow transformation in the mission of Jesus...So what is happening in this conversation between Jesus and the Canaanite woman is not that he makes an exception. It is a moment in a gradual turning of Jesus to the Gentiles."

But to the incident itself:

How dare this pagan woman shamelessly violate all protocol and yell out: "Have pity on me, Lord, Son of David! My daughter is tormented by a demon. But Jesus did not say a word in answer to her." Silence.

We may more than once sympathize with this determined woman. Surely she has consulted doctors and spiritual advisers and whomever, and nothing has cured her daughter. Jesus is her last resort, but he simply remains silent. As Radcliffe has it: "This silence is not a rebuff. He is silent because he is listening to her. It is rooted in his silent listening to his Father...It is the silence in which something new is germinating."

And this silence–hasn't this sometimes been our experience? Prayers, rosaries, novenas, daily Mass, and so on for ourselves or a good cause–nothing happens. Just silence. (As a young seminarian I remember making many a 9-day novena and basically saying at the last day: "It's been 9 days and I'd like to see some action here!")

In a word, bluntly, our pious props have failed us and we, with the pagan woman, sadly realizing the painful truth that "silence is the language of God." In the extreme, our strong inclination can be simply to give up on this God-thing and go it alone.

But not so the determined Canaanite who gives it another try: "(She) came and did Jesus homage, saying 'Lord, help me.'" Note carefully how the petition has changed! The first time, the emphasis was on her child: "My daughter is tormented by a demon." Now—and perhaps this is understandably the heart of the matter—she only says: "Lord, help me!"

The focus has clearly moved from the daughter to the mother herself. She, too, is hurting and needs healing just as much as does her daughter. After all her efforts, she has "hit bottom" with nowhere to turn. She feels abandoned. This may be our own situation at some point in our own lives.

But Simone Weil, the Jewish mystic, instructs and encourages us: "There should be nothing which distracts us from being alone at the foot of the Cross."

Eventually, after some verbal give and take, Jesus capitulates: "O woman ('My lady' is the better translation), great is your faith! Let it be done for you as you wish." Without knowing it, her unspoken prayer in faith was: "Thy will be done."

How often in our private and public places we have sung, mumbled or thoughtlessly parroted "Thy will be done!" In contrast, the Canaanite lady even now echoes the future words of Mary's faith: "Be it done to me according to your word."

What shouldn't be overlooked in this Gospel episode is that Jesus beautifully reaches out to the place, the role, the gift of all women. In our day, Pope St. John Paul II echoes the teaching of Jesus (*A Letter to Women*) written "to every woman, for all that they represent in the life of humanity" And he poignantly adds:

"Thank you, every woman, for the simple fact of being a woman! Through the insight which is so much a part of your womanhood you enrich the world's understanding and help to make human relations more honest and authentic."

IS GIVING OPTIONAL?

LUKE 10:30-37

Recently a college professor in Religious Studies invited me—sight unseen, and in my dotage—to address her class of 25 on the subject of altruism.

At the outset, and for my benefit, the students described their current altruistic projects, from working with the elderly to "random acts of kindness." My overall impression was that they generally view—like most folks—altruism (giving to others in a variety of ways) as something of a luxury: optional rather than obligatory, impulsive rather than consistent.

By contrast, Joan Chittister writes about hospitality is applicable to the virtue of altruism: she says that "it is not a series of grand gestures at controlled times. It is not a finishing-school activity. It is an act of the recklessly generous heart."

The Scriptures are saturated not with suggestions but with commands about caring for the helpless in society: widows, orphans, strangers, anyone without power.

Such directives would probably have been beyond these students, more interested in MBAs, pre-med and pre-legal studies. So I skipped such lofty ideals to offer a comparison that they could relate to: a brilliant flower in bloom.

For everyone, except those with severe hay fever, admire a colorful blossom. Its splendor, however, is short-lived. It is the stem that continues on with the important, quite unglamorous but lasting role. (Blossoms quickly come and go, but the stem remains!) The point is that the altruistic acts are the gorgeous colors that depend on a person's value system (the stem).

If, then, altruism is not going to be hit-and-miss incidents but a permanent feature of one's lifestyle, we have to look to, and nourish, our own character and Christian formation. Our goal, hopefully and with grace, is to learn and absorb virtues that will be permanent.

A true altruistic spirit must have a deep sense of compassion. Indeed. Joan Norris summarizes her stay with the Trappists: "Compassion is the strength and soul of a religion."

The parable of the Good Samaritan (Luke 10:30-37) remains as a concrete, practical example of what generosity implies. It is the opposite of a "scarcity mentality," today's prevalent attitude that in giving I may somehow be lessened: Compassion is sorrow + personal involvement.

The priest and the levite, both good clerics, obviously see the man in the ditch, but detour—note this—to the opposite side of the road. (At least they should have called 911!) Indeed, the literal meaning of "compassion" is "to suffer with."

Nor is true generosity naïve or blind; it is willing to take a risk even when there's a possibility of a scam. The Samaritan in the parable does not subject the helpless or needy person to an interrogation. He neither shames nor accuses the wounded man who, admittedly, should not have traveled alone and therefore asked for trouble. He does not scold: "You were a fool. It served you right." He does not blame: he sees a need and he acts.

Compassion is more than sympathy or empathy; it's not afraid to get its hands dirty in times of need. It does more than write a check, flip a dollar into the collection basket, hope that someone will do "something," or just feel sorry for the troubles of others. Compassion doesn't require words; it is not a sanitary, antiseptic virtue: its hallmark is being *with*.

There is no limit, no boundary to the object of generosity and compassion. The Good Samaritan parable addresses this directly when the teacher of the law asks: "Who is my neighbor?" Jesus startles the learned expert: "The one who was kind to him." Jesus said to him, "Go and do likewise."

Do you see the impact here? The lawyer (who actually represents all of us) rather smugly believes that *he* has the right to determine who his neighbor will be. But Jesus reverses it with the unspoken question: The man in the ditch is *already* your neighbor: can—will—*you* be his neighbor? The tables have been turned!

As Christians, indeed as human beings, we do not have the right to choose whom we will help. Love of neighbor, altruism, is simply not a luxury; it is a Gospel imperative. Generosity and compassion, the foundations of true altruism, often do not come naturally. They are learned; they need tending to, just as a plant's stem has to be nurtured and protected if it is to produce a blossom.

"Go and do likewise."

IT STARTS EARLY

NUMBERS 11:24

"Gang"—what's your first reaction? Probably people dealing drugs or certainly not up to anything respectable.

Not so! Everyone wants to be just a little bit different, while still identifying with a group. We find this desire throughout the Bible, even from the earlier books. Here is a classic example (Numbers 11:24-29):

> "So Moses ... gathered seventy elders of the people, and placed them all around the tent. Then the LORD came down in the cloud and spoke to him, and took some of the spirit that was on him and put it on the seventy elders; and when the spirit rested upon them, they prophesied."

Now the "gang" mentality kicks in:

> "Two men remained in the camp, one named Eldad, and the other named Medad, and the spirit rested on them; they were among those registered, but they had not gone out to the tent, and so they prophesied in the camp. And a young man ran and quite told Moses, 'Eldad and Medad are prophesying in the camp.' And Joshua son of Nun, the assistant of Moses, one of his chosen men, said, 'My lord Moses,

stop them!'

"But Moses said to him, 'Are you jealous for my sake? Would that all the LORD's people were prophets, and that the LORD would put his spirit on them!'"

The "gang" of seventy had their thunder, as it were, stolen. They wanted to be special.

We find the same kind of mentality in a New Testament incident (Luke 9: 46-50):

It's after the Transfiguration and Jesus is back with the people. But John has a problem: "'Master, we saw someone casting out demons in your name, and we tried to stop him, because he does not follow with us.' But Jesus said to him, 'Do not stop him; for whoever is not against you is for you.'" The "gang mentality!"

Now here's a contemporary situation: Apart from the notorious gangs of hoodlums roaming about today, with their horrible initiation rites, in our own sanitary way we, too, have our exclusions. In the annals of church history, for example, we read that "there is no salvation outside the Church." Taken literally and without explanation, this phrase gave a more than welcome elitist (gang) mentality: If you're not a baptized Catholic—forget it!

(But even in our own individual lives, we need to ask: Whom do I exclude from my church? From my circle of friends? Indeed, from within my own family? In all of us there is, somewhere, a trace of the "gang mentality.")

Today, though, there is an opposite and perhaps more dangerous problem that now pervades our society and our personal lives. Henri Nouwen (*Peacework*) describes it well:

"The greatest tragedy of our time is our isolation. Young children feel lonely and unable to find friends, adolescents band together to have some sense of belonging, young families don't know their neighbors. Men and women work in offices under neon lights, sitting behind metal desks, drinking instant coffee from paper cups, eating their lunch out of a paper bag, and often wondering if they make any contribution at all..."

St. Paul records his experience of isolation. His "conversion" is met with skepticism from the church leaders and he is told (Acts 9:9:30) in effect, "Don't call us—we'll call you." The laconic result is: "They took Saul to Caesarea and sent him away to Tarsus" where, for a long time, he has to ponder in isolation what is happening in his life. Later on, he again experiences the pain of separation, of being alone: "At my first defense no one appeared on my behalf, but everyone deserted me." (2 Timothy: 4:16) But on another occasion he heard the Lord's voice: "My grace is all you need. For my power is greatest when you are weak." (2 Corinthians 23:9)

And here is a contemporary model: John Henry Newman, beatified on September 19, 2010, by Benedict XVI. Probably one of the most renowned scholars and preachers in the Anglican world, long before his conversion he wrote these famous and telling lines:

Lead, kindly Light, amid the encircling gloom,
Lead thou me on!
The night is dark, and I am far from home,–
Lead thou me on!
Keep thou my feet; I do not ask to see
The distant scene,–one step enough for me...

What a wonderful prayer for us in times of puzzlement and darkness;

LEAD THOU ME ON!

IT'S JUST NOT FAIR!

MATTHEW 20:1-16

Most towns have what is called a Labor Exchange. You see it as you pass by every morning: a group of day laborers hoping that someone will hire them. The strong and muscular are picked up right away. For the next few hours the eager look at each car that stops and chooses a worker. By the end of the day there are usually a dejected handful of men just slumped over the picnic bench, despair in their eyes.

(In modern times I used to feel just like those losers: the image of a group of youngsters waiting to be chosen for the team. Invariably, and only out of sheer pity, I was always the last one. The shame of it all!)

This is the picture or parable that St. Matthew alone includes in his gospel. It's worth exploring.

Some fruits have to be picked at exactly the right time, at the peak of their ripeness. That's why the owner is determined to hire as many men as possible. Time is of the essence! So he returns again and again to the Exchange: he is desperate!

In fact, he is even willing to hire the few leftovers at 5:00 P.M. Money is no object for him. But who are they? Probably the lame, the puny. They are not lazy bums looking for a handout; They—and their wives and children—will go

---

hungry unless...

So here's the sundown situation that causes the bickering (to use a polite word): the owner or foreman reverses the payment process. The ones hired at 6:00 A.M. think that they should obviously be the first in line: "That's the way it's always done." (Reminiscent of us hungry seminarians standing in line for the after-school sandwich, an upper-classman could always say, "Class preference," cutting in line ahead of us urchins. That's the way it was!)

To make the point of the story more dramatic, the order is shouted: the last hired are the first to be paid! Not only that, they are to receive as much as the early birds! It's not fair!

"These last ones worked only one hour, and you have made them equal to us, who bore the day's burden and the heat." It's not fair!

Remember, though, that this story is a parable with a message. Precisely: the grumblers are victims of what M. Scott Peck dubs this diagnosis: "theomania." It's an attitude we're all susceptible to. We make assumptions, we have expectations of how God should be on our side, smoothly paving the way for us.

A tell-tale symptom of this attitude is the speediness with which we make comparisons. I try to be good, I say my prayers, even more than other people, and yet—why do I have disappointments, failures and suffering? It's not fair! You're in good company with Cardinal Hume:

> "I am now confessing to one of the biggest problems in my life: to know why. It is the biggest simple argument, for me, against the existence of God, I know all the answers, but I do not understand."

And even though he does not understand, he slowly, painfully, realizes that "it is only by looking at the crucifix that we can begin to discover some kind of solution...

because behind every crucifix you see, with the eyes of faith, the outline of the risen Christ. That is the point and that is why a crucifix is such a lovely thing."

And the supreme model for us is Jesus himself who prayed: "Father, if you are willing, remove this cup from me; yet, not my will but yours be done." When life is not fair, recall His promise:

"By your endurance you will save your souls."

IT'S NOT OVER YET

PSALMS 71-92

It's encouraging to hear these words from an older person: "Despite the limitations brought on by age, I continue to enjoy life." Pope John II continues: "Old age is the final stage of human maturity and a sign of God's blessing." (*Letter to the Elderly*).

People in the so-called prime of life may readily give an approving nod to these words which, for them, remain on the theoretical side. Seniors, though, may have some doubts. Society reinforces this with the attitude that the ability to produce and contribute to the economy is *the* driving force that gives meaning to life.

So there's a temptation, quite real, for older persons to pretend that they are younger than they look. Cosmetics are a big business! Surprisingly, that wise man, St. Augustine, spoke startling centuries ago:

"There is nothing so ugly as a person who never grows up or a sixty year old who tries to act like an adolescent. A human life is not meant to be a one note affair; it is meant to be a song. To have a melodic song every note must be sounded at its proper time and then passed on so that the next note can make its contribution. The beauty of the whole comes from the coming and going of each individual moment of sound. *So too the beauty of an individual's history comes from each moment of life occurring at its proper place and then disappearing forever into memory.*" (*Confessions*: 11:28)

If each life can be a melody, we friars hear it in the daily reading of the anniversary stories as they are recorded. Every deceased friar represents a life of faith and joy, despite failures as well as successes. They simply rejected society's demeaning attitude that old folks should be relegated to obscurity because they are no longer "productive."

As the psalmist proclaims:

"They are like trees planted in the house of the Lord, that flourish in the Temple of our God, that still bear fruit in old age and are always green and strong. This shows that the Lord is just, that there is no wrong in my protector." (92:13)

And more specifically, older folks can join the psalmist:

"You have taught me, O god, from my youth, and till the present time I proclaim your wondrous deeds. And now that I am old and grey, O God, forsake me not, till I proclaim your strength to every generation that is to come." (71:17)

Onward! Older people must embrace the key concept: "Each person plays the cards he holds and that is his adventure!" As he prayed for Peter, so the Lord prays for us: "I have prayed for you that your own faith may not fail; and you, once you have turned back, strengthen your brothers." (Luke 22: 32)

Oh, yes, there are the aches and pains that we seniors face daily. (When I awake in the morning, I check my body to see what's working and not working!). But Richard Morgan (*Autumn Wisdom*) offers a unique and comforting thought:

"I believe that on the cross Jesus experienced the diseases and infirmities of old age. On the way to the cross Jesus collapsed under the heavy wood, and although it was painful he got up and staggered to Calvary. He knew what it was like to be old and to fall down. He experienced loneliness, abandonment and rejection at Calvary, common experiences for older people. He knew *the painful feeling of remorse* over 'what might have been,' as do some older people who look back over their lives with regrets too deep for words."

"Jesus," he adds, "may not have reached a chronological old age, but he experienced old age in his body on the cross. *Ageless Christ, thank you for knowing what it feels like to be old. Amen*"

And Pope John Paul II gives us this beautiful prayer:

"Grant, O Lord of life, that we may ever be vividly aware of this and that we may savor every season of our lives as a gift filled with promise for the future. Grant that we may lovingly accept your will and place ourselves each day in your merciful hands. And when the moment of our definitive 'passage' comes, grant that we may face it with serenity, without regret for what we shall leave behind. For in meeting you, after having sought you for so long, we shall find once more every authentic good which we have known here on earth, in the company of all who have gone before us marked with the sign of faith and hope."

How almost coincidental are the words of the ancient church writer, Basil of Caeserea, who seems to have anticipated Pope John Paul's image of life as a passage. Basil's prayer echoes down the corridors of time to our own hearts:

"Steer the ship of my life, good Lord, to your quiet harbour, where I can be safe from the storms of sin and

conflict. Show me the course I should take. Renew in me the gift of discernment, so that I can always see the right direction in which I should go. And give me the strength and the courage to choose the right course, even when the sea is rough and the waves are high, knowing that through enduring hardship and danger in your name we shall find comfort and peace."

JONAH:
AN UNHAPPY PROPHET

THE BOOK OF JONAH

The fictional story of Jonah is a short book (reading time: 3 minutes!) with a simple plot: Jonah lives in an unnamed town – no other details are provided except that "The word of the Lord came to Jonah, son of Amittai"

Here's a man minding his own business when he is rudely, unexpectedly interrupted. His task: "Go at once to Nineveh, that great city, and cry out against it; for their wickedness has come up before me." It's a corrupt pagan city and Jonah wants no part of this so he buys a one-way ticket on a boat going to Tarshish (a mythical city) far away from the infamous, wicked Ninevah.

When a storm arises, the superstitious sailors question this stranger who admits that he is a Hebrew who worships the Lord. Panic sets in, "for the men knew that he was fleeing from the presence of the Lord, because he had told them so." Jonah, in an impulsive moment, suggests that they throw him overboard to appease their gods. But the crew defers and keeps on rowing until it's useless. "So they picked Jonah up and threw him into the sea; and the sea ceased from its raging."

All is not lost, however, for "the Lord provided a large fish (not necessarily a whale) to swallow up Jonah for three days and three nights." He prays to God for deliverance from this unusual townhouse. "Then the Lord spoke to the fish, and it spewed Jonah out upon the dry land," a relief to Jonah and probably even more so to the fish!

The Lord is persistent: "Get up, go to Nineveh, that great city, and proclaim to it the message that I tell you," a message of repentance. Jonah's heart is not in this so he wanders through the city, listlessly announcing: "Forty days more, and Nineveh shall be overthrown." To his utter amazement and disappointment the people heed the message and get down to the serious task of repenting. And God relents.

Jonah complains to the Lord, in effect, "I know that you are a forgiving God, so why did you send me on this useless journey?" In a snit he storms outside the city limits and sits down.

A nice touch: "The Lord God appointed a bush, and made it come up over Jonah, to give shade over his head, to save him from discomfort; so Jonah was very happy about the bush." For a while. The very next day God "appointed a worm that attacked the bush, so that it withered."

That's it – Jonah has had it and says: "It is better for me to die than to live." But God tells him in so many words: "Look, you're unhappy about your precious bush – shouldn't I be just as concerned about the people of Nineveh?" End of story. But it is also a story that deserves reflection.

While the principal and obvious thrust of this humorous short story is the universality of God's love in contrast to a narrow exclusivity — the premise that God only loves one nation (or only one religion) — there is a lesson applicable to our personal spirituality.

For example, Jonah did not want to be a prophet. Perhaps he had his own business concerns, his own goals, and felt unequipped for what God was asking. That happens to us: why at times does God seem almost to work against us? Anthony de Mello has a succinct bit of advice:

"In the game of cards called life one plays the hand one is dealt to the best of one's ability. Those who insist on playing, not the hand they were given, but the one they insist they should have been dealt – these are life's failures. We are not asked if we will play. That is not an option. Play we must. The option is how."

Jonah just doesn't get the message of God's universal mercy: "Should I not be concerned about Nineveh, that great city, in which there are more than a hundred and twenty thousand persons who do not know their right hand from the left, and also many animals?"

Later on, Jesus will tell the scribes and Pharisees (Matthew 12:41): "The people of Nineveh will rise up with this generation and condemn it, because they repented..." In our own day Pope Francis echoes Jesus:

"God never tires of forgiving us!...He never tires of forgiving us, but at times we get tired of asking for forgiveness, Let us never tire; let us never tire! He is the loving Father who always pardons, who has that heart of mercy for us all."

LONELY JESUS

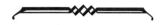

MARK 1:9

There are a couple of passages in the Gospel of that invite us to use our "active imagination" for meditation. We've probably heard about this, but it's good to remember the timeless advice of Cardinal Newman:

> "In a word, I wish to impress upon you, that our Savior's words are not of a nature to be heard once and no more, but that to understand them we must feed upon them, and live in them, as if by little and little growing into their meaning."

So after the introductory verses about John the Baptist these simple words begin our narrative: "In those days Jesus came from Nazareth of Galilee" (v. 9). He's about to leave everything with which he is familiar: boyhood friends and neighbors, his mother and his relatives, his job, a comfortable routine, the town itself. This must be a bitter-sweet decision and moment for him.

"In those days": there is no mention of traveling companions. Does he go by himself? Does he feel not only alone, but lonely as he turns for a lingering, last look at his home town? Has he made the right decision? Is he certain of this? Does he have friends or relatives waiting for him down yonder? Above all, does he have anyone he can talk with?

Unfortunately, it's easy to invoke the mystery: Jesus is both God and man and obviously knows everything past, present and future–no problem! However, St. Athanasius is already aware of this: "When viewed according to the flesh (he) lives within the limits of the human condition...*Viewed as an ordinary man, he does not know the future, for ignorance of the future is characteristic of the human condition...* For as upon becoming human he hungers, thirsts and suffers, along with all human beings, similarly as human he does not see the future."

Jesus hears about the "event" going on at the River Jordan. Mark simply notes that Jesus "was baptized by John in the Jordan." Why? Jesus is not play-acting: he is showing his solidarity with ordinary, fragile, sin-laden people.

Lamar Wilkinson (Mark) notes that the baptism is significant because, "as a secret epiphany, it tells the **reader** the true identity of Jesus.") Surely this was one a few "peak experiences" in his life. In our own lives we've had the occasional "peak experience" which helps us to carry on with our lives and ministries. Though they are few in number and quite transitory, these experiences do help us in the short rather than the long "haul."

For Jesus, the moment of exaltation is quickly over. "And the Spirit immediately drove him out into the wilderness." That ancient writer, John Chrysostom, remarks: "In this desolate place, the Spirit extended the devil an occasion to test him, not only by hunger, *but also by loneliness,* for it is there most especially that the devil assails us, when he sees us let alone and by ourselves."

How does Jesus cope with loneliness and model it for us?

All four evangelists make note of Jesus' habit of prayer: "They were especially taken with his apparent intimacy with God. The most extraordinary thing they noted in his manner and actions was his intimate and faithful union with his Father." (*Christian Community Bible*)

Second, this is not to say that Jesus is a loner! He dines with tax collectors and the occasional Pharisee. Above all, he cherishes the companionship of his twelve apostles and the mysterious one who is described as the "Beloved Disciple."

John's gospel (chapters 13 and 14) especially reveals his human need for intimacy and friendship and consequent concern: "And if I'm on my way to get your room ready I'll come back and get you so you can live where I live...I will talk to the Father and he'll provide you another Friend [the Holy Spirit] so that you will always have someone with you...I don't leave you the way you're used to being left—feeling abandoned, bereft. So don't be upset. Don't be distraught... Father, I want those you gave me to be with me, right where I am." (Peterson translation)

In speaking of loneliness. Pope Benedict XVI mirrored the importance of "church" in his own life as he spoke on July 25, 2005: "This should be understood from the outset: I will never again be lonely as long as I live. Faith redeems me from loneliness. I will always be supported by a community, but at the same time I must support the community and, from the first, also teach responsibility for the sick, the lonely, the suffering, and thereby the gift that I make is reciprocated.

"So it is necessary to reawaken an awareness of this great gift in the person in whom is hidden the readiness to love and to give himself or herself, *and thus guarantee that I too will have brothers and sisters to support me in difficult situations, when I am in need of a community that does not leave me stranded.*"

NAME THAT TUNE

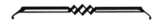

PSALM 137

"By the rivers of Babylon," writes the anonymous psalmist, "there we sat down and there we wept when we remembered Zion." (Psalm 137:1). The Lord has punished the people for their wicked ways with the ultimate, dreaded sentence: banishment from Zion (Jerusalem) to a foreign land.

The writer remembers the scene vividly. Lounging about, the Babylonians encourage the exiles to sing their traditional songs—and they refuse: "How could we sing the Lord's song in a foreign land?" (Reminiscent of the bored plantation owners asking the slaves to sing their hymns!)

The life and the theology of the Hebrews have an intimate expression in their music. In the entire Book of Psalms, for example—and thanks to computer wizardry!—"sing" appears 54 times and "song" racks up 47 mentions. Indeed, the psalms themselves are meant to be sung. More than anywhere else, Hebrew music captures and reflects their very identity. It's understandable, then: "How could we sing the Lord's song in a foreign nation?"

In their exile the people are depressed and confused. "Why, O Lord, do you stand far off?" (10:1) The question mirrors the real image of a sort of "divine amnesia"–a fear that God has simply forgotten them.

The honesty of these psalms invites us to reflect on the "exiled" times we experience in our own lives. *Mourning* is a pertinent example. There are both large and small moments—even weeks and months—when mourning is necessary and healthy, so much so that to repress our need to mourn may cause unconscious emotional unease.

Nor is mourning, limited to the death of a loved one. The realization that those wonderful childhood dreams have not materialized; that friendships can and do grow wane; that youth is irretrievably gone; that self-reliance and old age are frequently incompatible; that it may be time to surrender one's driver's license, even one's home: each person has a private, secret list of named and unnamed fears.

Unfortunately, we are expected to automatically tell people that "Everything's fine." Culture and society deliberately minimize mourning. But William McNamara asks: "What does it matter if in the past we have fallen or been neglected? What does it matter that we have been kissed or kicked, hugged or mugged?" Easier said than done.

Mourning and disappointment are often mixed with anger: "Where is this God of goodness in the midst of my sufferings?" The Hebrews are not the least bit reticent about shouting their anger in psalm 137: "Happy shall they (Babylonians) be who take your little ones and dash them against the rock!" That's pretty rough stuff, so much so that the Church unfortunately suppresses this verse in liturgical settings.

That's too bad, actually. For one thing C.S. Lewis writes, "The ferocious parts of the psalms serve as a reminder that there is in the world such a thing as wickedness and that it (if not its perpetrators) is hateful to God."

So, the exiled psalmist acknowledges his anger, expresses it and "gets it out of his system" by referring the whole messy thing to God.

It's more than merely "turning it over to God:" that could reflect a simplistic spineless dependency or cowardice. No, it's important for the psalmist to tell the Lord, often in detail, just how he feels about the helpless situation and God's apparent absence.

That's the value and the consolation of the psalms: they are so refreshingly honest! Joan Chittister notes: "One of the ways that the psalmist deals with anger is to face it in himself. It's amazing," she points out to us, "how we fear the anger within ourselves so much that we turn it against others by our chronic irritations."

By way of a healthy contrast, in good times and bad times the Hebrews still sing their songs: sometimes hymns of joy, at other times, songs of lamentations. Place yourself in St. Augustine's Easter Sunday congregation as he delivers an Easter homily in these splendid words that echo down the corridors of time to us:

"All you who have been born again in Christ and whose life is from above listen to me; or rather, listen to the Holy Spirit saying through me: *Sing to the Lord a new song.* Look, you tell me, I am singing. Yes, indeed you are singing, you are singing clearly. I can hear you. But makes sure that your life does not contradict your words. Sing with your voices, your hearts, your lips and your lives: *Sing to the Lord a new song*, and you wish to know what praises to sing. The answer is: *His praise in the assembly of saints*; it is in the singers themselves. If you desire to praise him, then live what you express. Live good lives and you yourselves will be his praise."

PARTY POOPER!

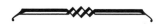

LUKE 15:11-32

As soon as we hear the gospel story of the Prodigal Son, "There was once a man who had two sons," our familiarity may cause our minds to wander off. "Been there, done that!"

The only expectation we have, and a dreary one at that, is the accompanying homily which either (a) tediously paraphrases the gospel; or (b) concentrates solely on the younger bad boy and the good father. "So," we ask ourselves, "what else is new?"

So enamored with the first part of the story, the priest or deacon rarely, if ever, gets to the older son who stayed home. Or, if he does, he simply dismisses him as being unimportant to the plot. Too bad—because "there's more to it than meets the eye." To refresh your memory with *The Message* translation (Luke 15:25-32):

"All this time his older son was out in the field. When the day's work was done he came in. As he approached the house, he heard the music and dancing." Recall that in his happiness the father was throwing a catered party for the wayward son, complete with live entertainment that obviously cost a pretty penny!

"Calling over one of the houseboys, he asked what was going on. He told him, 'Your brother came home. Your father has ordered a feast—barbecued beef!—because he has him home safe and sound.'" It's obvious that the servant could hardly wait to enjoy the reaction—he'd probably wanted to get a revengeful "dig" in for years. And he got his reward:

"The older brother stalked off in an angry sulk and refused to join in."

And he had, humanly speaking, every right to be outraged. His brother was arrogant and foolish, terribly selfish (selling his share of the property ate into the older son's inheritance), and left him with all the work to do. Who wouldn't be griped? But—a party? This was indeed the proverbial last straw.

"His father came out and tried to talk to him, but he wouldn't listen." And now it all comes out after years of repression: "The son said, 'Look how many years I've stayed here serving you, never giving you one moment of grief, but have you ever thrown a party for me and my friends? Then this son of yours who has thrown away your money on whores shows up and you go all out with a feast!'"

(Incidentally, at the top of the story we learned that the younger son spent his inheritance in "dissolute" or "riotous" living. There was no mention of prostitutes! Is this an example of "That's what I'd do if I had the chance?" Or as William Barclay pithily observes: "He had a peculiarly nasty mind.")

Scholar Tom Wright (*Luke for Everyone*) gives this succinct diagnosis:

"This story reveals above all the sheer self-centeredness of the grumbler. The older brother shows, in his bad temper, that he has had no more real respect for his father than his brother had had. He lectures him in front of his guests, and refuses his plea to come in."

It's easy for us also to blame the older son. But isn't he something of a mirror placed in front of us. How often do we hold resentments? What about downright envy of others? How sincere are our words of forgiveness? How about stubbornness toward others? The refusal to be open to other ideas, cultures, customs? We should not discount these personal questions.

But there is a wider issue in this parable because it was also directed at the Scribes and Pharisees—the church, as it were, of the day.

And they definitely realized that Jesus was saying that they were jealous of his inclusive love of the lowly and ritually unclean while they prided themselves on being "chosen," thanks to their strict observance of the Mosaic law.

What the *Christian Community Bible* says about the older son applies to them: "But the older son, the one who obeys, though with a closed heart, understands none of this. He has served with the hope of being seen as superior to others; and so he is unable to welcome sinners or to participate in the feast of Christ because, in fact, *he does not know how to love.*"

For us and our Church, then, "I tell you," Jesus says each day, "the angels of God rejoice over one sinner who repents" (Luke 15:10). That is our hope and our motivation.

PEOPLE OVER THINGS

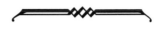

LUKE 12

As Jesus begins to speak, it's almost a mob scene. "As thousands of people crowded together, so that they were stepping on each other, Jesus said first to his disciples..." (Luke 12:1)

Here is a teaching situation that every teacher wants to avoid, but Jesus is doing his best. Granted that his immediate audience is relatively small ("Jesus said first to his disciples") others are pushing and shoving. In the middle of making a point, "Someone in the crowd said to him..." (v. 12) about an entirely different matter.

That statement should not go unnoticed because even Jesus experiences the irritation and the annoyance of being sidetracked. We call it "interruptions" and these happen constantly in our daily lives. We are intent on a project and someone always seems to want our attention, advice or company.

Granted that he is addressing his fellow Benedictine monks, Cardinal Basil Hume aptly captures this predicament:

"In everyday life we encounter all kinds of situations which are a constraint upon our initiative and our freedom in carrying out our tasks. Other people's plans, other people's arrangements, other people's ideas or quite simply, other people, frustrate us in one way or another. We are prevented from pursuing our ends, from carrying out our ideas as we would wish because there are others who have plans and ideas—or simply because there are others! This, I think, is what St. Benedict had in mind when he talked about being obedient to each other. He did not mean just taking orders from others: he means, rather accepting limitations which others impose on us by the very fact that they are 'others...'"

Jesus is our model here. Read through the gospels and notice how often people interrupt him, especially to argue and to criticize. And yet–he has time for these people even though their needs may be petty and extremely self-centered.

Case in point: The next part of the story (and only Luke records it) is a perfect example of how out of place an interruption can be: "Someone in the crowd said to him, 'Teacher, tell my brother to divide the family inheritance with me.'"

This brother is preoccupied with his own self-absorbed concerns. He hasn't been listening to Jesus. He is agitated because he feels that his brother is not following the traditional inheritance laws (prescribed by Numbers and Deuteronomy) Apparently he assumes that Jesus is not only respected but is a popular judge who will deal with an ugly situation. In his favor, of course.

This is by no means an unreal squabble. Many a family can vociferously testify to the bickering—the greed—that goes on before the decreased is even buried. (Sometimes it seems that the first phrases little tots learn, instead of "mommy" and "daddy," are "It's unfair!" and "I want my attorney!")

Once again, there is an unreal expectation dumped on Jesus. "Doing the will of my father" cannot and will not be reduced to sorting out degrees of selfishness. Jesus will not be a referee and he will not be sucked into this: "Friend, who set me to be your judge or arbitrator over you?" And he adds an important word to all the people watching the scene: "He said to them, 'Take care! Be on your guard against all kinds of greed; for one's life does not consist in the abundance of possessions.'"

The *Christian Community Bible* explains: "For though you may have many possessions, it is not that which gives you life," with the comment that "suppressing greed ingrained in our hearts is more important than looking at every person's right with a magnifying glass."

Basically Jesus is alluding to the deep fear that drives us to hoard material things. (One writer terms this an "immortality strategy.") Why are we driven to surround ourselves with not only necessary but superfluous goodies? "Maybe life seems so frail and contingent that many possessions are required to secure it," notes Lukan scholar L. Johnson, "even though the possessions are frailer still than the life."

Years ago an Italian novelist, Giovanni Guareschi (author of the delightful *Don Camillo* series) observed "moving day" for a family. Surveying the chairs and tables going into the van, he dubbed these material things "the crumbs of our existence." And so they are, and so they need to be seen in perspective.

Behind the human fascination with wealth, furnishings, toys, and assorted goodies is a denial of death. These things unconsciously take the place that God alone should and can have. Dietrich Bonhoeffer summarizes the matter tersely, bluntly:

> "Earthly goods are given to be used, not to be collected. Hoarding is idolatry."

Q'S THE NAME – LIFE IS THE GAME

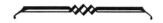

ECCLESIASTES

Perhaps the strangest book in the Old Testament (reading time: 10 minutes) is Ecclesiastes, best known for its opening words retained from the *King James Bible*: "Vanity of vanities! All is vanity!" (Modern translations: ("What a profound puzzle!" or "What a vast mystery!" or better yet (*The Message*): "Smoke, nothing but smoke!"

In the Catholic liturgy, passages from this book are rarely found. Why the neglect? Why, for that matter, did the ancients seriously debate as to whether or not it should even be included within the canon or list of inspired books, even though the author (commonly named Qoholeth or Teacher) believes in God?

Perhaps it's because the pessimistic author consistently denies any personal afterlife except Sheol. The late Scripture scholar, Roland Murphy states: "At first sight it would seem that the absence of a belief in a future life with God would present an inseparable difficulty in Christian prayer. Belief in a future life seems so central to Christian self-understanding."

Both the Book of Job and Ecclesiastes are "protest

books" that contradict, even deny, some of the Old Testament "wisdom" literature as, for example, the psalmist's blatant assertion: "I have been young, and now I am old, *yet I have not seen the righteous forsaken or their children begging for bread.* They are ever giving liberally and lending, and their children become a blessing." (37:25-26 NRSV) Job and Q would say: "Give me a break!" Or as Wilfrid Harrington remarks about that verse: "This is pathetic; a desperate clinging to a doctrinaire position in face of evidence" demanding that "you must sacrifice fact to theory."

In this tradition Qoholeth is a pragmatist, not a theologian or a philosopher. He just wants to make sense out of life independently of any afterlife. (As far as he is concerned, "The living know that they will die, but the dead know nothing; they have no more reward, and even the memory of them is lost." (9:5)

This is not to say that Qoholeth is an atheist—far from it. "I know that whatever God does endures forever; nothing can be added to it, nor anything taken from it; God has done this, so all should stand in awe before him." (3:14)

Having the money and leisure to do so, Qoholeth recounts that he's tried every conceivable pleasure; he's "been there, done that!" with thoroughness. All this, he says, is a "chasing after wind" (1:14), in other words, his argument is that life is so complex as to be beyond human understanding. His solution is simply to let go of our obsessions, take life as it is and enjoy the ride: "Even those who live many years should rejoice…yet let them remember that the days of darkness will be many. All that comes is vanity." (11:8)

On the positive side, Q offers a theology of work. William P. Brown comments in his fine book on *Ecclesiastes* that "the secret for Qoholeth lies in recognizing that one works not for self-gain, but **for the thrill of applying one's gifts and talents for the sake of another without any self-driven expectations of the results.**" (emphasis mine)

Yet far superior is wisdom: "Wisdom is as good as an inheritance... For the protection of wisdom is like the protection of money, and the advantage of knowledge is that wisdom gives life to the one who possesses it." (7:11-12)

But wisdom also has its limitations: "Whatever your hand finds to do, do with your might; for there is no work or thought or knowledge of wisdom in Sheol, to which you are going." (9:10)

So why read this somewhat depressing book?

Timothy Schehr notes:

"A significant contribution of this book is its lesson that we must become aware of how fleeting our time on earth is and act accordingly."

Martin Luther advised anyone in a position of administration to read Ecclesiastes once a week—for Qoholeth indeed sets all activity within the immovable boundary of life on earth. Carpe diem—seize the day! In Christian literature St. Paul would go further: "So whether you eat or drink, or whatever you do, do everything for the glory of God." (I Corinthians 10:31) And Qoholeth would wholeheartedly agree with Jesus: "Today's trouble is enough for today." (Matthew 6:34)

"The Christian has to admire the faith of the Israelites," writes Murphy. "They took God on God's terms: Sheol is the fate of all, good and evil alike. Many Christians tend to use personal eschatology (the future) as a crutch, but the idea of reward/punishment should not be allowed to dominate the outlook of faith.

His conclusion (emphasis mine):

"They lived with God in the present, and so must we even if we have a belief in a future life. It is the present that decides the future."

QUESTION:
WHO AM I?

MATTHEW 5:48

It's not uncommon, especially for a person over 40, to stop, seriously reflect on the past and present and reluctantly conclude: "I don't really know who I am." The accepted label for this is: "Identity crisis."

As a college senior I vividly remember the final comprehensive exam. The professor simply wrote on the board: Man. I suppose my learned ramblings were academically correct. But after 50+ years what I've learned is Man is a mess. And there are no exceptions." And this is true of the spiritual life, too.

More than once, everyone experiences the messiness of our life with God: call it an identity crisis, mid-life crisis, depression, spiritual emptiness, or the traditional "Dark Night of the Soul." Frequently this happens when we repeatedly face the stark fact that our failures far outweigh our successes in our life with God; when we feel no experience of Him; when prayer seems to be a total waste of time; when we thought that our sins and character flaws would change with time (They did—they become worse as we got older!); and finally, as a result, when we get to the point where we very seriously doubt whether God actually exists.

The big scriptural stumbling block is in Matthew 5:48: "You must be perfect—just as your Father in heaven is perfect."

For example, in his small, must-read classic, *Your God Is Too Small*, J.B. Phillips has a chapter describing God as "Absolute Perfection," or "the one-hundred-per-cent" God who demands "all or nothing at all."

Certainly we agree that God is perfect. But here's the trap, especially for perfectionists and introverts: Instead of taking random scripture verses in context, simply as parts of a whole, they invariably isolate individual texts and give them a meaning that actually was never intended!

The verse is actually the "bottom line" of Jesus' words about love of neighbor and enemies! Douglas R.A. Hare (*Matthew*) notes that the Greek—"must"—is in fact the verb's future tense and actually means: "You will be perfect" with no guarantees as to when!

But of vastly more importance is the question: what does "perfect" mean? If we take the word at face value, our experience more than adequately proves that we're in a hopeless situation. Jesus seems to be demanding something—perfection—that is far beyond us, saints included. (I like the old friar's solution: "Do what you can and can the rest.")

It's no laughing matter, though, for the sensitive soul; in fact, it's awful. Phillips explains: "But the conscientious, sensitive, imaginative person who is somewhat lacking in self-confidence and inclined to introspection, will find one-hundred-per-cent perfection truly terrifying. The more he thinks of it as God's demand, the more guilty and miserable he will become…" No wonder he often "breaks down" with a Christian identity crisis!

The way out is to understand what Jesus means by "perfect." In *our* language it means "entirely without fault or defect." In that sense no one can be perfect: if so, Jesus is commanding the impossible!

Luke's interpretation of this verse is: "Be merciful, even as your Father is merciful." (6:36) Our old translator-friend, Eugene Peterson (*The Message*), captures the true intention of the verse: "Live generously and gracious toward others, the way God lives toward you." And elsewhere: "Have integrity as God has integrity."

This command is an **ideal**. It is a goal amid and despite our daily failings. It involves a learning process: we have to **learn** how to follow in the footsteps of Jesus. Matthew is aware of this and reports Jesus saying: "Go and **learn** the meaning of the words..." (9:13) "Take my yoke upon you and **learn** from me." (11:29)

A colorful example is St. Paul, who certainly had a talent for messing up things in his life. He went through a religious identity crisis in his conversion experience. It really never changed his rambunctious, bold and sometimes petty personality. But with God's grace he finally realized: "My grace is all you need, for my power is greatest when you are weak." (2 Corinthians 12:9)

Peterson's translation captures Paul's memoir: "Once I heard that, I was glad to let it happen. I quit focusing on the handicap and began appreciating the gift. It was a case of Christ's strength moving in on my weakness.

"Now I take limitations in stride, and with good cheer, these limitations that cut me down to size...I just let Christ take over! And so the weaker I get, the stronger I become."

In our day Anthony de Mello sums the lesson up in a non-scriptural, down to earth word of advice:

"In the game of cards called life one plays the hand one is dealt to the best of one's ability. Those who insist on playing, not the hand they were given, but the one they insist they should have been dealt— these are life's failures."

Or, as Dag Hammarskjold (*Markings*) writes succinctly: "We are not permitted to choose the frame of our destiny. But what we put into it is ours."

QUIET, PLEASE!
I'M IN CHURCH

MATTHEW 21:30

Catholics of an earlier generation knew the rubric: Once you enter the church: no talking, laughing or other human distractions. The church building is a sacred place! You've come to talk to God! Silence, please!

A not-so-subtle change has come about. Nowadays people who arrive early for the scheduled Mass chat, gossip, wave to one another and just have a glorious time. Not only is there tacit approval from many priests, but the pre-Mass activity is aided and abetted in churches by the instruction that everyone stand and greet one another ("the community") before the procession begins: sort of a general "howdy-doody" completed later on by what one writer describes as "the embarrassing and theatrically insincere 'sign of peace.'"

As a priest admittedly of "the earlier generation," I sometimes long for the old-time "silence in church." For instance, while I was standing, vested, in the rear of the church, the chorale singing, the altar servers in place, an usher sidled over to whisper urgently: "There's no toilet paper in the bathroom." Good grief—both for me and for the parishioner-in-agony.

But I think I am having, not a conversion experience, but a change of heart about the pre-Mass activity.

"My house was designated a house of prayer; you have made it a hangout for thieves." (Matthew 21:13. Peterson tr.)

Yes, but Jesus' objection *on that occasion* does not seem applicable today. An interesting argument about this comes from Libby Purves, a columnist in *The Tablet*. She writes:

"A brief human interaction before divine proceedings always seems to me a kindly affirmation that churchgoing is not only a matter of worshipping the invisible but of gathering together in a spirit of goodwill."

She goes on to make a fine point:

"We are getting on, a lot of us live alone, and for some of us Mass is the only time we regularly get out of the house and meet a lot of friends all together. It's too cold to stand outside and talk. So we murmur to one another in the minutes before Mass. What's wrong with that?"

She elaborates further:

"Doesn't God want elderly parishioners to be kind and thoughtful and sociable and interested in one another's ailments and descendants? Doesn't He like the idea of two young mothers under his roof murmuring a supportive mutual greeting before the serious praying starts?" In a word: "Doesn't God like the human race?"

Maybe we need to remember the distinction between private prayer and communal or liturgical prayer. We can "do" our personal devotions anywhere, and, I suggest, carrying them out in the church before Mass doesn't add any particular heavenly weight to them.

But once we enter the church, we are individuals affirming that we, too, are the People of God with all the idiosyncrasies and annoyances of people everywhere.

Perhaps we can temporarily abandon our personal boundaries and find the Lord not only in the tabernacle—with the red lamp—but in all those wonderful, disorganized, sometimes lonely and bewildered strangers around us.

Perhaps the Lord values our reaching out to other worshippers even more than he listens to our private prayers in those pre-Mass moments. The key may well be compromise: let each person respect another's space in the nave.

Regardless of present practices and preferences, then, the over-riding goal has to be:

"How very good and pleasant it is when kindred live together in unity" (Psalm 133:1)—or as Peterson's homey translation has it: "How wonderful, how beautiful, when brothers and sisters get along!"

REACHING OUT

LUKE 6:6

"No good deed will go unpunished." That is a cynical saying–but experience sadly proves its truth. Certainly it is frequently a fact for Jesus as he goes about teaching and healing.

Just one of many examples is when he enters the local synagogue on a Sabbath day. The Gospel of Luke (6:6-11) describes the incident:

"On another Sabbath Jesus went into a synagogue and taught. A man was there whose right hand was paralyzed." Notice how observant Jesus is: it's the right hand, not the whole arm.

Besides the regular congregation there is an added attraction: "Some teachers of the Law and some Pharisees needed a reason to accuse Jesus of breaking the religious law, so they watched him closely to see if he would heal on the Sabbath."

There must be some unspoken excitement here, not only because Jesus has become a kind of celebrity, but also because "the big guns" from out of town are in attendance.

The Lord isn't intimidated by his "distinguished guests." "But Jesus knew their thoughts and said to the man, 'Stand up and come here to the front.' The man got up and stood there." Apparently he's in a back pew (reserved for the poor) and is reluctant to move up to the front—perhaps he is afraid, not only of the unknown, but because he has become the unwelcome center of attention. Maybe he's a deliberate "plant" to attract Jesus' attention.

Now Jesus seizes a teaching moment publicly aimed at the authorities:

"I ask you: What does our Law allow us to do on the Sabbath? To help or to harm? To save someone's life or destroy it?" Silence.

He looks around the congregation and says to the man, "Stretch out your hand. He did so, and his hand became well again."

No applause. But the congregation must be snickering with delight. Once again, and with no apologies, Jesus has basically insulted the Establishment: "They were filled with rage and began to discuss among themselves what they could do to Jesus."

Parenthetically, William Barclay (*Daily Study Bible*) draws a contemporary application: "There is an ever present danger of setting loyalty to a system above loyalty to God... There is in this story a glorious atmosphere of defiance. Jesus knew that he was being watched but without hesitation he healed. He bade the man stand out in the midst. This thing was not going to be done in a corner."

"Stretch out your hand." The first instance of reaching out is in Genesis 3:6-7:

"The woman saw how beautiful the tree was and how good its fruit would be to eat, and she thought how wonderful it would be to become wise. So she took some of the fruit (stretched out her hand) and ate it. Then she gave some to her husband, and he also ate it."

And the 4th Gospel closes with the poignant words of Jesus to Peter and to us:

"I am telling you the truth: when you were young, you used to get ready and go anywhere you wanted to; but when you are old, you will stretch out your hands and someone else will tie you up and take you where you don't want to go."

For ourselves, we are called daily to stretch out our arms to the Lord. How? In a striking commentary, St. Ambrose (c. 340-397) gives a detailed application:

"You heard, then, the Lord's words: 'Stretch out your hand.' Here is the cure for us all. And as for you who believe your hands are clean, beware lest avarice and beware lest sacrilege paralyze it. Stretch it out frequently: stretch it out towards the poor man who is begging you; stretch it out to assist a neighbor, to bring help to a widow, to rescue from injustice someone you see to be subjected to undeserved humiliation; stretch it out towards God for your sins. This is how our hands are stretched out; this is how they heal."

Sadly but certainly we fail, we become discouraged in ourselves and in our obligation to reach out, to stretch our horizons. So the advice of Pope John Paul II gives us welcome hope and strength:

"Christian holiness does not consist in being free from sin, but in seeking to fall as few times as possible, and then rising again after each fall." (*On Our Pilgrimage to Eternity*).

RESTORING SHALOM

So you think you have mastered your impatience and maybe your anger–permanently? Try using an advanced computer! Or even better: buy a new software program, race home with it because the label—every software label—boasts without qualification: "User Friendly." Ha!

One thinks of the psalm: "Honest people can no longer be found...All of them lie to one another...Silence those flattering tongues!" (12:1-3)

But experienced persons are wary of those grandiose promises. More than once they've seen their computer freeze up in protest against an alien invasion. So they know exactly what to do *before* they face another disaster: Use the RESTORE button! It returns the computer to "where it was" before the intrusion of that cantankerous piece of software. And all is well again!

Jesus knows well what "restore" means, and it's signified in one small word: "Shalom," commonly translated as "Peace!" It's a greeting that has almost become trite because it is open to a variety of interpretations.

But consider how Jesus uses "Shalom:" Following the resurrection, his first words to the distraught disciples are:

"Peace (Shalom) be with you!" (John 20:19). Shalom! He does not say, "Where were you when I needed you?" or "Thanks a lot, fellas!" Just: "Shalom!"

No reprisals, no sarcastic words here. When Jesus says, "Peace be with you," he is actually saying: "Let's carry on where we left off–that good and wonderful relationship between us in days gone by." Restoration! Broken, unhappy relationships are swept aside: "Shalom!"

Some days later he reinforces this by Lake Tiberias when he greets the disciples: "Young men, haven't you caught anything yet?" And after the miraculous catch, "they saw a charcoal fire there with a fish on it and some bread." Jesus is barbecuing! What a splendid example of "Shalom"–friends having a picnic!

Lots of people (maybe you and I) are a bit leery or skeptical about this notion of Shalom. It can be a problem for us, aided and abetted, even encouraged, by many a sermon and dour "spiritual reading" book, to say nothing of a parental warning: "God is watching you!"

J.B. Phillips (*Your God Is Too Small*) calls this learned idea of a fearful God the "Parental Hangover:"

> "If he (the child) is lucky, he will outgrow this conception, and indeed differentiate between his early 'fearful' idea and his later mature conception." However, he sadly notes: "But many are not able to outgrow the sense of guilt and fear, and in adult years are still obsessed with it, although it has actually nothing to do with their real relationship with the living God."

Phillips is right on the mark! From my 50+ years' experience as a priest, I am totally convinced that the life-task of most Catholics is to study and contemplate the true image of God so often emphasized by Jesus:

"My Father will love whoever loves me...I love you

just as the Father loves me; remain in my love." (John 14, 15)

Or even those simple words: "Our Father, who art in heaven." When will we begin to realize, to make the magnificent discovery, that the Fatherhood of God should not, must not, be based solely on our experiences of human parents?

In our journeying toward spiritual maturity we make mistakes. But God's Shalom is with us all the way. St. Paul is profoundly aware of this: "The one thing I do, however, is to forget what is behind me and do my best to reach what is ahead. So I run straight toward the goal in order to win the prize, which is God's call through Jesus Christ to the life above. All of us who are spiritually mature should have this same attitude." (Philippians 3:13-15)

What better expression of God's Shalom is this prayer of St. Francis who, in his own journey of spiritual restoration, could eventually pray:

You are love, charity; You are wisdom, You are humility,
   You are patience, You are beauty, You are meekness,
   You are security, You are rest,
   You are gladness and joy, You are our hope, You are justice,
You are moderation, You are all our riches to sufficiency.

You are beauty, You are meekness,
   You are the protector, You are our custodian and defender,
   You are strength, You are refreshment. You are our hope,
   You are our faith, You are our charity,
   You are all our sweetness, You are our eternal life:

Great and wonderful Lord, Almighty God, Merciful Savior.

SHALOM!

SALVATION:
WHAT, INDEED,
IS IN A WORD?

GENESIS 49:18

In our culture, we are so bombarded with words that we begin to lose their original meaning. A simple example: why do we use the word "gala" for a joyous party? We may be surprised that it actually comes from the word "guillotine" when a whole town would gather to watch an execution!

Even in religious language, words acquire different meanings in the course of time. Take the simple word, "salvation." It occurs at least 643 times in the Bible, beginning with Genesis 49:18: "I wait for your salvation, O Lord." Here Jacob is pleading for deliverance from his enemies. Nothing about eternal life!

So *Eerdman's Dictionary* is able to devise a broad or generic definition of Old Testament salvation: "God's deliverance of a people from a threatening situation from which that group or person is unable to rescue itself," always with God in the background. The Old Testament is sprinkled with this notion:

"Come quickly to help me, my Lord and my salvation." (Psalm 38:22) "My salvation shall not tarry." (Isaiah 46:13) "In the Lord, our God, is the salvation of Israel." (Jeremiah

3:23) There is no reference to life after death. But the Jewish people certainly believed in "salvation" from a variety of here and now perils. As for a future life, the ancients took life as it is and tried to make the best of it under God's law. So says Ecclesiastes: "The best thing a man can do is eat and drink and enjoy what he has earned." (2:24)

Or as Peterson (*The Message*) has it: "The best you can do with your life is to have a good time and get by the best you can."

Coming to the New Testament, there is a dramatic shift in the meaning of salvation: personal life after death now comes to the forefront (over 40 instances): "He has raised up a horn for our salvation," (Luke 1:69)… "Salvation is from the Jews" (John 4:22) "For our salvation is nearer now than when we first believed." (Romans 13:11)

Oh, yes—we Christians rightly continue to use the word "salvation," but its impact escapes us. No one expects the imminent end of the world. We are content. We have our creature comforts. There is so much of nature that can be controlled. True, we blithely chirp "and for us and for our salvation" in the Creed every Sunday, But it can be rather meaningless in our *café latte* culture. Alexander Schemann vividly explains:

> "Salvation presupposes that one is perishing. A drowning man, a man whose home is engulfed in flames, a man falling over the edge of a cliff does not pray for comfort or comforting words, but for *salvation. Yet it is just this sense of perishing, and therefore the experience of Christianity as salvation, that has been suffocated over the long centuries of Christianity.*" (Emphasis mine).

In fact, he starkly notes: "All of this we confess when we say the simple and eternal words of the Symbol of faith: 'For us men and for our salvation.' For us, for me, for you, for each of us individually and for all of us together, for our salvation. Every time we repeat this affirmation we affirm also our knowledge of destruction. Many would like to remove from Christianity this link between salvation and destruction, salvation as a result of destruction."

Destruction?

"This substitution has taken place because *we have stopped viewing ourselves as beings who are truly perishing,* beings whose life is rushing inexorably toward meaningless collapse, whose life is engulfed by evil, by senselessness, by the horror of dying and death, by the bestial struggle for survival, by the terrible lust for power, by the war of all against all, by lies which poison the very sources of life, by ignorance and by the universal sentence of death…"

That's why the final verse of the *Benedictus* (Luke 1:78-79) is such a great prayer of faith in salvation and the first definition of the human condition in the Gospels:

In the tender compassion of our God the dawn from on high shall break upon us,
to shine on those who live in darkness and the shadow of death,
and to guide our feet into the way of peace.

The vast majority of Christians continue out of habit to say words such as "Savior," "salvation," "save us," but within themselves they now unconsciously experience these words in a different way than did the early Christians. Within Christianity itself a peculiar substitution of words has taken place, or rather, not of words, because the terminology stays the same, *but of meaning, how the words are heard.*

All of this we have somehow learned not to notice, while still recognizing that it is very frightening to live. All of this we have learned to charm away by the frantic pace of everyday life…*This is a humanity which is afraid to stop, afraid to reflect, afraid to be alone with itself* and to see that destruction, fear, hatred and evil are the very life to which we are condemned.

Yet this is exactly the awareness, the image of life, that is found in the Gospels. Christ comes to a people who are "sitting in darkness" and "in the shadows of death." It takes no more than a minute's reflection to recognize that this has always been and always is: that **destruction tyrannizes the world and dominates life**. If one does not realize this, if one does not begin with this awareness, then Christianity makes no sense and has really nothing to say to anyone.

It is only in disclosing the depth and horror of this destruction that Christianity discloses itself, or more accurately, discloses Christ—His teaching and His call—as salvation. Salvation not from this or that, but salvation of life itself, so hopelessly torn away from its own proper content—from God, from light, from heaven, from Truth, from eternity—a life which has become, in this broken state, a terrifying, stinking swarm of human beings all equally condemned to senseless destruction.

It can be said that **every genuine encounter with Christ first of all discloses to me the darkness, the destruction, the senselessness of my life**. I see Christ, and because I see Him, I understand that the life I live is not real life, but a life which is permeated with destruction...

And my faith in Him, in Christ, begins with this: that in a manner mysterious and inexplicable, yet so self-evident, I recognize that only He, Christ, can save me, that only with Him and in Him do I find salvation for myself, for other persons, for everyone, for everything.

SIGNPOSTS ALONG THE WAY

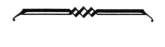

GENESIS 28

Here's something that most of us are familiar with:

You park at the airport or in a mall, not paying all that much attention to where you have parked. An hour later, loaded with bags, you come back But—where exactly and in which lot did you leave your car?

And the search begins. You wander about but don't want anyone to know your plight. So "Joe/Jane Cool" is your embarrassed attitude—pretending that you actually know where you are going! Ah, yes—we've all been in this modern-day labyrinth!

Perhaps we can take a helpful hint from the story of Jacob (Genesis 28:15ff). On his journey to Haran he spends a night under the stars, using a stone for a pillow. In a dream he is visited by the Lord who promises:

"I will be with you and protect you wherever you go,
and I will bring you back to this land. I will not leave
you until I have done all that I have promised you."

Jacob realizes two things: First, The Lord appears to him–not in the temple, not while he is praying, but in the wilderness. He wakes up and exclaims: "The Lord is here! He is in this place and I didn't know it."

We can often relate our prayer-time with a certain spiritual wilderness that descends on us every now and then. Sister Wendy (*Sister Wendy on Prayer*) vividly says that "it can be very hard to stay in this state of powerlessness, of blindness, of vulnerability accepted." But her advice is encouraging: "Prayer is impossible without trust...Feeling or non-feeling are equally unimportant." And this is the wisdom for all of us who experience troubles and helplessness and struggles when prayer almost seems, frankly, to be a waste of time.

Second, following this divine visitation, Jacob must continue his journey before returning to his homeland; he needs a signpost to point the way back. So: "Jacob got up early next morning, took the stone that was under his head, and set it up as a memorial...." He goes on to explain: "This memorial stone which I have set up will be the place where you are worshipped."

Signposts can be a most valuable aid for us, particularly when we pray the Scriptures. There are unexpected verses that often strike us deeply when we are meditating. These are meant to be underlined, cherished and revisited.

Ronald Knox, in the preface to his translation of the psalms, speaks from his own experience: "Most of us have had, at some time, lights of our own in reciting the Office; or verses quoted in books of meditation or in retreats will have stuck in our minds so that we hail them, when we come across them again, like a man greeting an old friend."

In the story of Jacob there is another message. After a long time, when he returns to face Esau, the brother he had flagrantly deceived years ago, Jacob is afraid of retribution, revenge. He needs to sort things out in his own mind. So he sends his family ahead of him. But more: "After he had sent them across, he also sent across all that he owned, but stayed behind alone."

Alone. Alone, that is, to come to grips with his own

feelings and to pray that Esau will forgive him. Not an easy task, but one that only he can face–until a mysterious man "came and wrestled with him until just before daybreak."

For our own spiritual lives, there is a lesson here. Our life, our journey, just doesn't happen: it requires faith and surrender, struggling with God. When we have these "down times"—and we will have them—we can identify with the groaning of the Old Testament psalmist (44:23-26):

Wake up, Lord! Why are you asleep? Rouse yourself! Don't reject us forever!
Why are you hiding from us? Don't forget our suffering and trouble!
We fall crushed to the ground; we lie defeated in the dust.
Come to our aid! Because of your constant love, save us!

The Scriptures are replete with encouraging words— signposts—for us when we experience darkness—maybe months, years—when prayer just seems to be a monologue and we are left with silence. The *Letter to the Hebrews* (4:16) urges: "Let us have confidence, then, and approach God's throne, where there is grace. There we will receive mercy and find grace to help us just when we need it."

Above all, we cling in faith and hope to the words of Jesus (John 14:1ff) who assures his Twelve and, through them, each of us individually:

Do not be worried and upset...Believe in God and believe also in me. There are many rooms in my Father's house, and I am going to prepare a place for you...And after I go and prepare a place for you, I will come back and take you to myself, so that you will be where I am.

(Scripture citations are from *Today's English Version*)

STANDING STILL

MARK 10:46

Interruptions—welcome to the world of Jesus! How often we read in the gospels that people want to argue, others want immediately attention, many need instruction. And Jesus only has 2-3 years of public life!

How does he handle all these distractions and intrusions? There's a secret here that Mark's gospel (10:46) offhandedly tells us: "Jesus stood still." See how it works in this story:

"They spent some time in Jericho. As Jesus was leaving town, trailed by his disciples and a parade of people, a blind beggar by the name of Bartimaeus, son of Timaeus, was sitting alongside the road. When he heard that Jesus the Nazarene was passing by, he began to cry out, 'Son of David, Jesus! Mercy, have mercy on me!'"

"Jesus stopped in his tracks. 'Call him over...' Throwing off his cloak, he was on his feet at once and came to Jesus. "Jesus said, '**What can I do for you?**' The blind man said, 'Rabbi, I want to see.' 'On your way,' said Jesus. 'Your faith has saved and healed you.' In that very instant he recovered his sight and followed Jesus down the road." (*The Message*)

He does not say, "I'm too busy" or "I've got other things

on my mind" or "I can't be bothered." These thoughts are understandable: he is deliberately moving toward Jerusalem where he will face the showdown of his life...and death. But: **"Jesus stopped in his tracks."**

This probably doesn't sit well with the disciples, the "insiders," while Bartimaeus is definitely an "outsider," even though the gospel writer mentions his name and background. Jesus, however, doesn't play favorites: every person is an individual and therefore unique. (*And how often do we choose who deserves our help? Or are we simply content to absolve ourselves by putting something in the offertory collection? Or worse: Do we simply pretend that we are momentarily blind?*)

There's an instructive sidebar here:

"Bartimaeus came like a shot when Jesus called. Certain chances happen only once. Bartimaeus instinctively knew that. Sometimes we have a wave of longing to abandon some habit, to purify life of some wrong thing, to give ourselves more completely to Jesus. *So very often we do not act on it on the moment—and the chance is gone, perhaps never to come back.*" (Charles Barclay: *The Daily Bible Study*)

There are several other reflections in this incident for our consideration...and meditation:

Bartimaeus knows *exactly* what he wants and is not afraid to cause a scene in the process. So intense is he that he throws off his cloak—the most valuable day-and-night apparel that anyone has in those days. (*And we: how lethargic and vague our prayers can be, And how little we are willing to sacrifice for the Lord?*)

Bartimaeus, knowingly or unknowingly at that moment, will have to change his lifestyle if he receives his sight. No longer can he sit by the roadside with his beggar's cup! He will have to get a job! (*And when we pray, are we willing to listen to the Lord's desires for our lives? A life of "contemplation" includes action—work, too!)*

Blasé Pascal makes the point: "All the troubles of life come upon us because we refuse to sit quietly for a while each day in our rooms."

Jesus is our model as we read in the gospels how often Jesus prayed by himself. For example, "When Jesus heard the news about John, he left there is a boat and went to a lonely place by himself...After sending the people away he went up a hill by himself to pray." (Matthew 14:13;23) "At once the Spirit made him go into the desert, where he stayed forty days." (Mark 1:12)

All four gospels are sprinkled with details similar to these. And add the grand promise: "And I will do whatever you ask for in my name, so that the Father's glory will be shown through the Son. If you ask me for anything in my name, I will do it." (John 14-13) But first:

Stop in your tracks!

SUCH A COMMON WORD

PSALM 69:16

In recent years the "buzz word" has become popular. Especially do we murmur "low self-esteem" for bad behavior as, for example, "he/she committed the crime because of low self-esteem." The ideal goal, obviously, is a constant state of high self-esteem.

It's encouraging, though, to have M. Scott Peck (*The People of the Lie*) critique the matter: "In order to be good, healthy people, we have to pay the price of seeing aside our self-esteem once in a while, and so not always feel good about ourselves."

A person who buys into the high self-esteem mania will have a difficult time with the Bible, especially the Hebrew Scriptures (Old Testament). It's there that over and over again we encounter the cry for mercy. (Indeed it is found 214 times!) At face value, self-esteem doesn't have a chance!

There's a solution here, if you think it through. It doesn't require a college degree to realize that it is not only possible but quite common for a word to have several legitimate, respectable meanings. Take the word "order:" it can be a noun ("I gave the order") or as verb ("I order you"). A single world can have, as it were, several offspring. "Play" can refer to a stage production, frolic, card games, etc.

Precisely here is the essential distinction that must not be overlooked. In a word: context. Back to the word "mercy:" Mark Borg is absolutely correct when he observes: "Granted, sometimes mercy and merciful do appear in biblical *contexts* where the issue is sin and forgiveness. In such *contexts* they are good translations. *But because of the common meaning of mercy and merciful today, they are many times not good translations.* (*Speaking Christian*. Emphases mine.)

Let just one simple biblical verse stand for many similar ones: "Have mercy on me, O God...according to your abundant mercy blot out my transgressions." (Psalm 51:1) God is the subject and David is the object because he has sinned. In other words, "mercy" implies that there is one (God) who has power to forgive and one (the sinner) who receives the benefit (absolution) Surely the context is clear, and "mercy" is the appropriate translation.

But why does Borg maintain "many times not good translations? Once again, and risking the boredom of repetition, look at another verse *where no removal of sin is implied*: "When he hesitated, the men, by the LORD'S mercy, seized his hand and the hands of his wife and his two daughters and led them to safety outside the city." (Genesis 19:16)

So how shall "mercy" be translated? What does it mean here? The answer: compassion. There are countless scriptural references—contexts—where "compassion" is more exact and appropriate than "mercy." Keep this as a thumbnail guide: mercy ON, compassion WITH.

Here are several approved translations of Psalm 69:16:

"According to your abundant *mercy*, turn to me." (NRSV)

"In your *great compassion*, turn towards me." (REB)

"In your *tenderness* turn towards me." (NJB)

"In your abundant *kindness*, answer me." (NABre)

In your reading of the Bible, if you understand that "mercy" always and exclusively implies that you've been bad, bad, bad, then obviously your self-esteem is zapped.

But if "mercy" quite often joyfully describes the divine compassion, the tenderness and the kindness of God, we gradually begin to interiorize the psalmist's song (103):

Praise the Lord, my soul!
All my being, praise his holy name!
Praise the Lord, my soul,
And do not forget how kind he is!

THAT WORD AGAIN

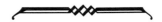

MATTHEW 22:35

Sometimes it's just one thing after another. Jesus has had a set-to with the Sadducees (a small but respected group who base their beliefs primarily on the first 5 books of the Hebrew Scriptures). This is an opportunity not to be missed: "When the Pharisees (which eventually came up with 613 commandments) heard that Jesus had silenced the Sadducees, they came together" to use what they consider to be a trump card in the game called "Gotcha!"

Douglas Hare (*Matthew*) describes a popular belief that "since all commandments are of equal importance in God's eyes and are to be observed solely for God's glory, it is sinful to argue that some are more important than others on the basis of some merely human standard of judgment."

So here's the no-win argument the Pharisees plan. "Teacher," one of them asked, "which is the greatest commandment in the Law? Sounds innocent, but here's the answer Jesus gives: Besides loving the Lord, which is "the greatest and the most important commandment," he immediately adds a second: "Love your neighbor as yourself" and "The whole Law of Moses and the teachings of the prophets *depend on these two commandments.*" That reluctantly satisfies his opponents, since, as Hare notes: "Implied is a similarity in the theological depth and interrelationship."

Whether it refers to God or neighbor, just what does the over-used word "love" mean in our everyday lives? We mouth it so often that perhaps it has lost its true biblical understanding: commitment.

The Lord gives us, in his kindness.

THE LOVES IN OUR LIVES

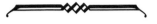

ISAIAH 3:18-19

Remember the song, "Some Enchanted Evening?" There is something quite touching about "young love" because, for many, this may be the first time they have experienced unconditional love, love without strings attached.

This temporary feeling brings with it a certain blindness. The danger, the infatuation, blocks the reality that the couple do not—cannot—really see. And that is their strengths and weaknesses. When this is kindly pointed out, their basic explanation is: "We love each other."

And that is the genius of the various churches' "Engaged Encounter," and why a 3-month (or so) instruction time is required. The purpose is to help the couple to see each other *as they really are* (besides being a "cooling off" period). Of course, a reluctant couple may object, "Don't worry–things will be different after we're married." (How true...and how sad!)

There is a great, almost overwhelming power in the experience of unconditional love because often a person has never experienced it to this point in their life. Repeatedly as children they heard such phrases as: "Why can't you be like..." or "You're just like..." or "If you get better grades...or the real clincher: "God is watching you."

"God sees you." An older man relates how he was visiting an even older lady who had a plaque on her living room wall: "God Is Watching You."

As he stared at it, this wise lady saw the look on his face and said something that changed his whole life. The explanation was simple but profound:

"God sees you with such great love that he simply can't take his eyes off of you." No condemnation, no accusation—just perfect, permanent unconditional love, no matter what.

But what truth does Scripture proclaim in hundreds of passages? Listen to the parable of the so-called prodigal son's return (Luke 15:20): "This son of mine was dead, but now he is alive; he was lost, but now he has been found." No conditions, no recriminations.

Basil Hume has something so touching about love, so remarkable for its intimately personal candor:

"I want someone to know me completely, to understand me entirely, and someone to want me unconditionally. **I want to be somebody's first choice**, and I think the only one who knows me completely, understands me entirely, and wants me unconditionally, is God—**and I am his first choice; and you are his first choice.**

The marvelous thing about God is that he cannot have second choices. He is limited that way! We are all first choices. God never sees crowds, he just sees the individuals."

Those are the words of a monk, an abbot and finally a Cardinal of the Church who went up to his quarters after his grand reception as archbishop of London...and cried. He was lonely. And so he wrote these sustaining, encouraging words, without knowing that he was bequeathing them to you and to me:

"So we are all his first choice and only he can give what I truly need and truly want: that unconditional love which is totally satisfied and totally complete, and I know I will only realize that when I see him face to face. **Meanwhile I can speak about it, have doubts about it, have a glimpse of it, then it clouds over again.** That is the rhythm of life. But I have got to hang on to the fact that all the time, whatever my mood, whatever my attitudes, whatever my failures, I am his first choice..."

"When, however, the Spirit comes,
who reveals the truth about God,
he will lead you into all the truth."
(John 16:13)

THE MAN WITH ALIASES

ACTS OF THE APOSTLES: 1

*The Old Testament (and religious orders until recently!)
bestowed a new name upon a person chosen for a new way of
life. St. Paul (a.k.a. Saul!) echoes this custom in the emphasis
on baptism being death and rebirth to a new life.*

An interesting example of this in The Acts of the Apostles
is "Joseph called Barsabbas, who was also known as Justus."
(Acts 1:23). The context of this occurs with the intention to
replace Judas Iscariot so that the number 12 will remain
intact.

In conducting job interviews, the eleven apostles have
one primary criterion: the candidate must be "one of the
men who have accompanied us, beginning from the baptism
of John until the day when he was taken up from us–one
of these must become witness with us to his resurrection."
(21-22)

The two finalists are the above mentioned Barsabbas and
one Matthias. It's interesting that the former is thoroughly
identified, but the other, Matthias, has only one name! The
author of The Acts of Apostles isn't big on biographical
details.

How do you choose between two equally qualified

persons? No employer in our society would solve the issue by rolling dice or picking high cards out of the deck! That is generally not considered to be an acceptable, professional approach.

"But amongst the Jews," one writer explains, "it was the natural thing to do because all of the offices and duties in the Temple were settled that way. The names of the candidates were written on stones; the stones were put into a vessel and the vessel was shaken until one stone fell out; and he whose name was on that stone was elected to office." So it comes to pass:

"And they cast lots for them, and the lot fell on Matthias; and he was added to the eleven apostles." (26) How does Barsabbas feel about being passed over? Anger? Embarrassment? Sadness? Depression? And we: how do we feel and react to a similar situation when we are not so much passed over but even ignored?

Comparisons can and does often start at an early age beginning with kindergarten! Have you ever been the last one chosen for a team of any kind? Have you felt the lack of praise from a teacher? Perhaps a lack of affirmation even at home ("Why can't you be like your brother?")

For example, a successful man now in his seventies wrote a book of published poems. One is about his father–a good man who loved his children but was unable to express his feelings. And now this elder son, long after his father's death, alludes to this conscious lack of affirmation in a poem significantly titled, "I Wanted To Share My Father's World:"

"...and even now I feel inside
The hunger for his outstretched hand,
A man's embrace to take me in,
The need for just a word of praise."

The writer? President Jimmy Carter. Like so many, many other men and women, he felt sort of passed over or compared to other boys...and has carried that burden, that cross, all of his life! And let us not forget how often we give aliases based on comparisons—by word, attitude or action— to older folks, titles like "senior citizens" and "old-timers," frequently forgetting that they have names, stripping them of their individuality.

Aliases are no substitute for what the Old Testament especially refers to (26 times) as the opposite: "integrity," "But as for me, I walk in my integrity" (Psalm 26:11); "Whoever walks in integrity walks securely" (Proverbs 10:9); "He walked with me in integrity." (Malachi 2:6). And in the New Testament we read: "Show yourselves in all respects a model of good works, and in your teaching show integrity" (Titus 2:7). No aliases!

Our tasks, then, are twofold: first, to rid ourselves of our hidden, even subconscious aliases that we present not only to the world but especially to God. Second, to be vigilant that others do not attach labels (aliases) to us.

Job's goal must become ours: "Until I die I will not put away my integrity from me." (Job 27:5) What a prayer—and it must be ours!

THE OLD AND THE NEW

Few Catholics remember the rubrics (=liturgies) before Vatican II. Recently, someone gave me a *Missale Romanum* (Roman Missal) that, like the Lone Ranger, took me back "to the days of yesteryear."

What specifically brought memories was the Mass for the Dead. The vestments were black, the organ was permitted only to "sustain" the choir (usually one person), flowers were absolutely not allowed on the altar or anywhere else, the coffin was unadorned, the accompanying prayers were dramatically stark and vivid (*"Dies irae, dies illa,"* in English: "The day of wrath, that day!")

Perhaps this strikes a contemporary person as ghoulish and depressing. But there were elements in its favor. Bluntly: you knew that the person was dead and the mourners were not allowed to forget that. Today we prefer antiseptics such as "passed on," or "We lost so-and-so." The old rite left no doubt about it: the finality of death was the focal point. More than an invitation, there was virtually a demand that the mourners and reflect on their own mortality.

For Vatican II (*The Church in the Modern World*) teaches succinctly that "the enigma of the human condition becomes greatest when we contemplate death. Man suffers not only from pain or the slow breaking-down of his body, but also from the **terror of perpetual extinction**. It is a sound instinct that makes him recoil and revolt at the thought of this total destruction, of being snuffed out. He is more than matter, and the seed of eternity he bears within him rebels against death. All technical undertakings, however valuable, are powerless to allay man's anxiety; prolonging his span of life here cannot satisfy the desire for a future life inescapably rooted in him."

However, the "old rite" was not all gloom and doom. To be sure, most of the prayers begged forgiveness for the deceased. But there were strong elements of hope. Think of the magnificent *In Paradisum*:

"May the angels lead you into paradise;/ may the martyrs come to welcome you/ and take you to the holy city,/ the new and eternal Jerusalem."

Still, this whole business of grief, dying and death is something we readily and habitually push aside. Pope John Paul II (*Letter to the Elderly*) wrote: "Death thus forces men and women to ask themselves fundamental questions about the meaning of life itself." At a funeral home I remember delivering the sermon (=homily) for a deceased mother and mentioning that any funeral is a graced moment for all of us to think about our own values: Where we've been, where we are going. Suddenly, and especially startling for me, one of her adult sons, somewhat intoxicated, blurted out for all to hear: "Did she put you up to this?" It took about two sentences for me to conclude the service!

Today we tone down the whole funeral formalities. We speak of "The Mass of the Resurrection" and wear white vestments. The music is perhaps overly joyful (If I hear "On Eagle's Wings" one more time...) A somber sermon has been replaced or augmented—to the secret dismay of many a celebrant—with sometimes interminable personal eulogies and recollections. But each liturgical style has its own strengths and weaknesses.

Regardless, St. Gregory Nazienzen offers this poignant prayer for us: *"And meanwhile let us commend to God our own souls and the souls of those who, being more ready for it, have reached the place of rest before us although they walked the same road as we do...*

"And receive us too at the proper time, when you have guided us in our bodily life as long as may be for our profit. Receive us prepared indeed by fear of you, but not troubled, not shrinking back on that day of death or uprooted by force like those who are lovers of the world and the flesh. Instead, may we set out eagerly for that everlasting and blessed life which is in Christ Jesus our Lord. To him be glory for ever and ever. Amen."

And Saint Pope John II:

Grant, O Lord of life, that...we may savor every season of our lives as a gift filled with promise for the future. "Grant that we may lovingly accept your will and place ourselves each day in your merciful hands. And when the moment of our definitive "passage" comes, grant that we may face it with serenity, without regret for what we shall leave behind. For in meeting you, after having sought you for so long, we shall find once more every authentic good which we have known here on earth, in the company of all who have gone before us marked with the sign of faith and hope.

"Mary, mother of pilgrim humanity, pray for us "now and at the hour of our death." Keep us ever close to Jesus, your beloved Son and our dear brother, the Lord of life and glory. Amen."

THE SOUNDS OF SILENCE

LUKE 9:35

In the Simon and Garfunkel album, *Sounds of Silence*, there is a memorable line: "People talking without speaking/ People hearing without listening."

Parents and teachers often ask a child: "When will you learn to listen to me?" And they're right—listening is a learned art! S&G hit it right: all around us, people hear... but they don't listen.

The Holy Spirit urged the same message at His Son's transfiguration: "A voice said from the cloud, 'This is my Son, whom I have chosen–listen to him.'" (Luke 9:35) And more than once Jesus—with good reason—tells his disciples and the crowds: "Listen, then, if you have ears." (8:8) Even the prophets complained: Isaiah in his disgust laments that the people are "always refusing to listen to the Lord's teachings." (Isaiah 30:10)

A common example demonstrates the difference between hearing and listening: people in the airport boarding area read books, doze off or talk to each other–all kinds of sounds fill the air. Suddenly the desk attendant announces: "Those of you who are waiting for the delayed flight..." At that point passengers are definitely listening, not just hearing!

To another situation: are people hearing but not listening when the Liturgy of the Word is proclaimed during the Eucharistic celebration? As a presider I sometimes wonder about this. To be sure and realistic, there are obstacles. Quite often a selected reading stands alone: it is taken out of context (something like reading the middle chapter of a mystery–you don't know what went on in previous pages and therefore the passage does not seem to make sense. And let's not even mention St. Paul's letters!) Or possibly the sound system is inferior and of poor quality. And, to be frank, some lectors are untrained and monotonously read words rather than "sense lines."

This "hearing without listening" often pervades our own personal prayer life. Take a moment to examine how you pray: Isn't it often the case that we do the talking and don't give the Lord a chance to respond? In a reflective pause we can almost hear the Lord pleading: "Give me a break–I'd like to get a word in here, too."

Cardinal Carlo Martini in his marvelous book, *Jacob's Dream*, speaks of discernment in prayer which he describes as "an exercise in attention, in listening to the Spirit of God in our soul in order to grasp the divine will in its direction of our life."

But the crucial question is: do we want a change of direction? Maybe that is why we are content to pray "on the surface" of our minds. We fall into a trap: we say prayers... but we are not praying. We feel safer and more comfortable offering words to the Lord rather than being still and listening to His word.

Martini rightly goes further; "Discernment is listening to the *unwritten word of God,* which even today resounds freshly and uniquely in the consciousness of the faithful." While "it is true that whatever the Lord is saying generally to humankind, the Bible is valid also for the individual. *But scripture does not supply that utterly unique word that I am seeking...No one is able to hear this word for me."* (Italics mine)

In his own life he acknowledges that the Word can come even during routine activities, but he confesses that "as a general rule, I recognize this particular word of God for me in a spiritual climate and activity, within the setting of the life if the Spirit."

This "climate" is both necessary and invaluable in the Jewish tradition. Rabbi David Wolpe says that "in some peculiar way, prayer is always moving toward, but never quite arriving, at silence." In this healthy tradition where words are terribly important, "the worshipper must *hear* his or her words." An interesting Jewish thought: "To speak words buried inside do not have the force of words that have been heard, even if they have been heard only by the ears of the speaker."

All is summed up in the words of the psalmist:

"If today you hear the voice of the Lord, harden not your hearts." Or in Peterson's translation: "Drop everything and listen, listen as he speaks: don't turn a deaf ear." (95:7-8)

THE TWO MARKS

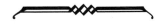

MARK 14:40-51

The name of Mark appears in the gospels describing the arrest of Jesus. But there is a difference:

"Then all the disciples left him and ran away." Matthew 26:56) "They arrested Jesus and took him away." (Luke 22:54) "Then the Roman soldiers with their commanding officer and the Jewish guards arrested Jesus, tied him up and took him..." (John 18:12) It's Mark's gospel that adds a curious detail: "Then a the disciples left him and ran away. A certain young man, dressed only in a linen cloth, was following Jesus. They tried to arrest him, but he ran away naked, leaving the cloth behind." (14:51)

Who is this biblical streaker? Some say that he is actually the writer of the Gospel of Mark. However, biblical scholar Garrett Galvin says unequivocally that we do not know the names of the gospel writers. "If you look at the books in Greek, there is nothing indicating the names of the gospel writers."

While the authorship is unknown, why does the inspired writer make a point of highlighting this minor, hardly significant detail? John R. Donahue (*The Gospel of Mark*) answers: "In the Bible nakedness is a sign of shame...In leaving behind him his *sindon* (linen cloth) the young man chooses shame over fidelity to Jesus," perhaps an allusion to Adam and Eve hiding in the bushes.

Bishop Tom Wright also writes (*Mark for Everyone*): "Are we ready to betray Jesus if it suits our other plans, or if he fails to live up to our expectations?" And he broadens the point: "The Church is called to live in the middle of this great scene: surrounded by confusion, false loyalty, direct attack and traitor's kisses, those who name the name of Christ must stay in the garden with him until he Father's will is done."

This name of Mark comes up later ("...he (Peter) went to the house of Mary, the mother of John whose other name was Mark. (Acts 12:12) So now we have a John Mark, the future missionary companion of Paul and Barnabas. We read: "Then after completing their mission Barnabas and Saul returned to Jerusalem and brought with them John, whose other name was Mark." (12:24)

So far, so good! When the missionaries came to Perga in Pamphylia, *"John, however, left them and returned to Jerusalem."* Why? Is he sick? Or just homesick? Later on, Paul is still fuming: "Barnabas wanted to take with them John called Mark. But Paul decided not to take with them one who had deserted them in Pamphylia and had not accompanied them in their work. *The disagreement became so sharp that they parted company. Barnabas took Mark with him and sailed away to Cyprus. But Paul chose Silas and set out..."*

How sad! We surely find Paul's rigid stance less than edifying. Where is the forgiveness he had preached in Romans 13? *The Christian Community Bible* does temper this judgment: "The sudden breakup between Paul and his friend Barnabas should not surprise us: faith does not destroy one's personality. But time and thanksgiving tend to lessen conflicts." And it did take time, a long time for Paul to get over his resentment against John Mark until we read such verses as:

"Aristarchus, my fellow prisoner greets you, as does Mark, the cousin of Barnabas..." (Colossians 4:10) and elsewhere: "Only Luke is with me. Get Mark and bring him with you, for he is useful in my ministry." (2 Timothy 4:11)

Like Paul we may have resentments that can't be forgiven instantly. It may take time for healing. So we pray with Paul for God's grace (I Corinthians 13:1ff. *The Message*):

Love never gives up.
Love cares more for others than for self...
Love doesn't want what it doesn't have...
Doesn't force itself on others...
Love doesn't strut, doesn't have a swelled head...
Doesn't keep score of the sins of others...
Puts up with anything, trusts God always...
Never looks back, but keeps going to the end.

WHAT SHOULD *YOU* DO?

MATTHEW 5:23

There's nothing like a flamboyant person to attract a crowd.

After "the word of God came to John, the son of Zechariah in the desert" (Luke 3:2) there's no stopping him from making enemies–he has a knack for explosive words: "You brood of vipers! How will you escape when divine punishment comes?" Subtlety is not one of his endearing qualities.

Whether serious or mocking, some in his audiences want answers to his order: "Produce now the fruits of a true change of heart." Concretely, what does this mean? So he lays it out for them:

First, he addresses everyone in general: "The people asked him, 'What are we to do?'" Cutting through pious instructions he is quite clear: "If you have two coats, give one to the person who has none; and if you have food, do the same." Hoarding, consumer mania, toys and trinkets, narcissism—the list goes on—and we in our American culture tragically continue to buy into materialism with a vengeance.

Then—and this is a bit surprising—"even tax collectors

came to be baptized and asked him, 'Master, what must we do?'" Hated as they are by everyone, he doesn't tell them to give up their despised occupation: they, too, have to make a living. But that's no excuse for bribery and cheating. "Collect no more than your fixed rate." Hard-heartedness and plain old greed effectively block or at best postpone any idea of repentance. (And what do we compulsively hold onto in our lives?)

Next in line are the military: "What about us? What are we to do?" Are they asking cynically? No matter. John lays it on the line, pinpointing their abuses: "Don't take anything by force or threaten the people by denouncing them falsely. Be content with your pay." (How we subtly pressure others into doing what we want! And gossip has become an art form!)

So John has spoken to 3 groups of people. What is missing here? The well educated clergy and the scribes (attorneys) of the day, the influential professionals ones who unashamedly flaunt a sense of superiority over "the peasants!" (Aren't we often in the same categories as we practice innocuous, comfortable religion or, to cite Dietrich Bonhoeffer, settle for "cheap grace" which he describes as "grace without discipleship, grace without the cross?")

Note that in each of his directions, in modern terminology, John's advice is not to go to Mass more often, say the rosary daily, make a pilgrimage to Lourdes or have a pious doo-dad on the dashboard of our family chariot. John says nothing here specifically about religious practices or, for that matter, the popular notion of "religion."

John's concern, indeed his demand, is with justice and forgiveness. He is trying to pound in the idea that there can be no true religion, no real love of God, without these virtues. Don't bother with prayers, he is saying, unless you interiorize and "do" justice first.

Jesus echoes this: "If you are about to offer your gift at the altar and there you remember that your brother has something against you, leave your gift there in front of the altar, go at once and make peace with your brother, and *THEN* come back and offer your gift to God." (Matthew 5:23).

"What shall I do?" is not identical with the faddish question, "What would Jesus do?" In many situations we frankly don't know what Jesus would do! What is important and essential is that no one, from Pope to Scripture, can give me an answer to my personal situation and "What shall I do?" in my life. Priest-psychologist Josef Goldbrunner once explained:

> "To live a spiritually healthy life one must find one's own truth...One must consciously come to terms with the irrational forces within oneself." He rightly concludes: "When the soul does not live its own truth, the vision of God's truth becomes clouded." And we find our truth through consistent prayer, silence and meditation. These are available to each person *if the will is there."*

WHAT'S THIS ALL ABOUT?

MARK 3:20FF

Time for a bit of detective work about a puzzling, curious passage tucked away in the Gospel of Mark, considered to be the earliest written gospel. Here are his recollections about a particular incident:

Jesus has made his new home in Capernaum which serves as a base for his itinerant preaching missions. He has made friends and enemies. Especially enemies.

Rumors about him have spread all over, including Nazareth. "The Pharisees went out immediately and conspired with the Herodians against him, how to destroy him." Two separate incidents seem to be reported:

First: "When his family heard it, they went out to restrain him, for people were saying, 'He has gone out of his mind'" (Mark 3:20-21 NRSV). A secondary reason in these perilous days is the possibility of "guilt by association."

Then: "His mother and his brothers came; and standing outside, they sent to him and called to him." (3:31)

This is a troublesome detail for avid Marian fans who will quickly assume that she is merely an onlooker and that, because she is Jesus' mother, she somehow has inside knowledge about her Son's vocation. Basically, and even though well intentioned, this does a disservice to her as a human being and mother. Old-time Catholics—myself included—lived through the great Marian Age of the 50s and 60s and were accustomed to the "Avon Lady" statues of Mary: always serene, collected and—certainly—in perfect agreement with whatever her Son says or does.

So, in this view, when the boy Jesus was found in the Temple, the implicit explanation is that Mary knew all along where He was, but asked this question for our edification. We don't take seriously the stark remark: "But they did not understand his answer."

In the understandable desire to honor Mary, it isn't easy for us to picture her burning a meal, becoming cross at times, potty-training her Son along with all those details of family life. Scripture merely records the understatement: "His mother treasured all these things in her heart." Like all mothers, she knows her Son is special—but that's about the extent of it.

To put it another way: If from the outset Mary knows the entire salvation scenario, where are faith and hope in her life? Somewhere St. Augustine states firmly that Mary's glory is not in being a mother but, rather, in being the first disciple!

This is no easy task for Mary or for ourselves as disciples. Romano Guardini (The Lord) gives us a description of what this entails:

"God is before us, more real than anything else, and yet He is hidden. He is seen by the inner eye of faith; He is known by the heart which loves Him. But the inner vision is often clouded and the heart is dull; thus we have no immediate experience of God. *Communion with Him through mere faith, reached as it were through the emptiness and darkness of the unknown, is extremely difficult.*"

Mary had to walk in the darkness of faith until the

Resurrection. And as our Mother also, she is with us in our journey:

Hail, holy Queen, Mother of mercy, hail, our life, our sweetness and our hope. To thee do we cry, poor banished children of Eve: to thee do we send up our sighs, mourning and weeping in this vale of tears. Turn then, most gracious Advocate, thine eyes of mercy toward us, and after this our exile, show unto us the blessed fruit of thy womb, Jesus, O merciful, O loving, O sweet Virgin Mary! Amen.

WHEELING AND DEALING

MATTHEW 25-43

Parables seem designed not only to tell a stories but deliberately to leave the audience puzzled and, hopefully, discovering more than one message. Check out this particular situation that Jesus tells the people about the Kingdom of Heaven:

"For it is as if a man, going on a journey, summoned his slaves and entrusted his property to them; to one he gave five talents, to another two, to another one, to each according to his ability. Then he went away. (A talent was worth more than fifteen years' wages of a day laborer. We're not talking small change here!)

"...each according to his own ability."

The generous donor knows the abilities of each man. By giving them different amounts, there is no idea of punishment or insult. He simply knows their strengths and their weaknesses. He respects these differences.

(Jesus graciously treats us according to our individual personalities (abilities): introverts and extroverts, saints and sinners. To each and every person he lovingly grants the exact grace for finding, obeying and loving him.)

"Then he went away." Notice that the owner does not give

the three men instructions about what they should do with their talents! He allows them to use their own ingenuity. He simply treats them as mature adults.

"The one who had received the five talents went off at once and traded with them, and made five more talents. In the same way, the one who had the two talents made two more talents."

Eventually the owner returns and congratulates these two for investing his talents and doubling them. He rewards them with more responsibilities.

This gives us pause to think about the graces God has offered us. Are we content simply not to commit sins? Or is the Lord going to ask us: "Very well, but what good have you done?" I have never forgotten the person who sincerely told me: "I'll be happy just to get to Purgatory." Is that the purpose of grace?

Which brings us to the third person who is given one talent:

"Master, I knew that you were a harsh man, reaping where you did not sow, and gathering where you did not scatter seed; so I was afraid, and I went and hid your talent in the ground. Here you have what is yours."

So he believes that the owner is "a harsh man." But the other two had no issue here. Where did the idea of harshness come from? Possibly from his earliest days when an authority figure (father, for example) was a demanding person. I remember Sr. Joan Chittister remarking somewhere that, in the vowed life, when a sister cannot get along with any superior, it is probably that she is actually but unconsciously rebelling against her own father (who may be long dead)!

This third man is therefore afraid of taking a risk of investing his talent and seeing the market go down. But true growth, natural or spiritual, always implies uncertainty, the possibility of making a mistake, Or maybe this man is just plain lazy. Fr. Anthony Giambrone, O.P. explains:

"If the third servant makes out badly...it is because he has rendered his portion from the Lord *closed to growth*...He has not even left the talent to increase in the bank—a thing requiring no effort from him. His hole-in-the-ground investment strategy has positively cut off all possibility of increase."

There may be an objection here, borrowed from the business world: "The rich get richer and the poor get poorer." But Giambrone's point is that the third man is "closed to growth." And that principle holds for the spiritual life also. A person open to spiritual growth will indeed grow, but if he doesn't make the effort, God's grace cannot prevail.

So Giambrone prays: "Father in heaven, break down every obstacle I have put to your grace. Let your generous kindness overwhelm me with good favor that I might become ever richer and richer in your blessings."

This holds for all of our lives! We are to take the risk of surrendering in faith to God even though we cannot see the future. As we friars of the St. Barbara celebrate our 10th anniversary this year, we, too, gladly invest in the future. There's a wonderful, powerful prayer by Blessed Cardinal Newman who was a fellow traveler with you and me:

O my Lord, and Savior, in your arms I rest secure. If you keep me, I have nothing to fear; but if you abandon me I have nothing to hope for. I have no idea what will happen to me as I await my death; I know nothing of what is to come; but I entrust myself to you. I lean entirely on you since you know what is good for me. As for me, I do not know. Amen.

WHEN PRIORITIES GET LOST

HAGGAI: 1

After decades of Babylonian exile, it is a pagan emperor, Darius, who invites the Israelites back to Jerusalem. But what the excited old-timers, who were just kids when the deportations took place, don't know is that their beloved country has not only been ravaged, but even more tragic, their glorious, spectacular temple of Solomon is no more.

So their excitement and eagerness are totally devastated when they stare at their barren land: everything wiped out! Well—life must go on!

With determination they clear the rubbish, rebuild their homes and plant their crops. But something's not right...and God explains:

"You have sown much, and harvested little; you eat, but you never have enough;" and perhaps worse, "you drink, but you never have your fill." (Or as the TEV translation says drolly: " You have wine to drink, but not enough to get drunk on!")

One of their own, the prophet Haggai, speaks in behalf of the Lord who is a bit miffed: "My people, why should you be living in well-built houses while my Temple lies in ruins?" There's the rub: the people's priority has been with their own busyness and they have ignored the Lord and his desires.

(How often all of us fall into the identical trap of being anxious about not only necessary things but with our own ease and amusement? How often, at the end of another hectic day, do we reflect: "Where has the time gone?" and with it the realization (hopefully) that we have neglected any conscious contact with God).

Off the folks go:, chopping down trees, heating up the forges, paying artisans and architects, contracting with metal workers and all the rest. Finally, they finish—behold the Temple!

How to describe it? Awesome, stunning, impressive? On the contrary. Despite all the hard labor and sincere goodwill, the old-timers just shake their heads as they sadly recall the old, glorious temple. But this new "thing" is "the pits." They're downcast, shamefaced and discouraged.

(That's about the way we feel—or perhaps should feel—about our own spiritual "house," our spiritual life. As we get older, our personal histories get longer and we see them stained with broken resolutions, unfulfilled dreams, long-term habits we're ashamed of, the constant stream of temptations—so many disillusionments!)

The Lord understands how they (and we) feel: "Is there anyone among you who can still remember how splendid the Temple used to be?" (Sage heads nod) "How does it look to you now? It must seem like nothing at all." (Emphatic nodding.)

At this point the Lord reminds the downcast folks: "When you came out of Egypt, I promised that I would always be with you." This is a key concept in Jewish (and our) history: The Lord keeps his promises, he stays with the people and never abandons them.

In fact, all Jewish theology is summarized in two brief verses of psalm 103: "The Lord is merciful and gracious, slow to anger and abounding in steadfast love. He will not always accuse, nor will he keep his anger forever." (v. 8-9)

Gazing, perhaps amusedly, at the pitiful new Temple and the silent people, the Lord speaks these marvelous lines through Haggai: "But now don't be discouraged, any of you. Do the work for I am with you...I am with you, so do not be afraid."

Can you hear these confronting, strengthening words knocking at the door of your heart? Yes—we become discouraged at our lack of progress; yes—sometimes we feel abandoned and solitary; yes—sometimes especially because of illness or the race of time itself, we feel unwanted, neglected.

It is faith—often sheer faith in darkness—that helps us to hang on: "I am still with you, so do not be afraid." It matters not whether (as Cistercian William McNamara puts it) we've been hugged or mugged, kissed or kicked. What matters is that we are indeed a new creation, that we are no longer orphans but friends of the Lord, and that there is a special destiny for each one of us because we *are* unique.

Cardinal Newman captures it all when he offers the prayer: "The night is dark; and I am far from home—Lead thou me on!" And though we've had our dark moments and have fallen into life's potholes, there is the promise that "with the morn those angel faces smile, which I have loved long since, and lost awhile."

A FRIAR'S AUTUMN

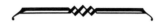

You may think past ages were good,
but it is only because
you are not living in them.
ST. AUGUSTINE

Early one Fall morning—the sun was barely hinting at a smile—I was walking along the driveway at St. Francis Retreat. Idly I glanced down—and there it was: a leaf that had floated, quite modestly, to the ground, demurely waiting for a bit of companionship.

It was astoundingly, delicately beautiful, offering a silent moment *to catch sight from time to time of what is truly real. It is no more than a flicker of light through the cloud of unknowing...*(Basil Hume)

What might this bronze and golden leaf murmur? Would it complain: *Now is the winter of our discontent?* (Richard III) Or perhaps an encouraging reminder:

The night is nearly over, day is almost here...
Let us conduct ourselves properly,
as people who live in the light of day. (Romans 13:12)

A leaf on the ground: a graced symbol! Its very loveliness timidly, but surely, affirmed its individuality. Within a multitude of leaves it was–well, both distinct and special. It's very presence affirmed the glory of all creation:

*Every person born into this world represents something new, something that never existed before, something original and unique...Every man's foremost task is the actualization of his unique, unprecedented and never-recurring potentialities, **and not the repetition of some that another, and be it even the greatest, has already achieved.*** (Martin Buber)

Lying there on the road, the leaf's brilliant but now dimming colors mirrored the rains and the storms, the joys and the fears of the past. But it had weathered these!

Lift up your tired hands, then, and strengthen your trembling knees! Keep walking on straight paths, so that the lame foot may not be disabled, but instead be healed. (Hebrew 12:12 TEV)

That and other leafy jewels invite, beg us to pause, to listen, to learn:

The falling leaves are subtle reminders that we are asked to let go of many things throughout our life. Every time we must surrender something we connect with our death, with the ultimate moment of letting go. (Joyce Rupp)

Scripture is well aware of this:

When you were young you dressed yourself and went wherever you wished,
    but when you get old you'll have to stretch out your hands while someone else dresses you
        and takes you where you don't want to go.
(John 21:18, Peterson tr)

How, then, do we—friars—willingly approach the senior years? With curiosity and dignity, a sense of elán and delightful creativity? Or, quite sadly, depression, a feeling of uselessness, of being overlooked and unappreciated?

The psalmist, who appreciated nature's vegetation, encourages us to be like trees:

That still bear fruit in old age and are always green and strong. (Psalm 92:14)

An anonymous commentary adds that "The life of faith does not deteriorate or wear out...There is a flourishing of faith that comes to its most lively expression in the later years. **We are called to move from success to significance."**

Faith!

An interlude: There, in the center of St. Peter's Basilica, feeling utterly desolate and discouraged, I glanced up and vividly saw—way up above—the Gospel words in mosaic tile:

Rogavi pro te ut non deficiat fides tua.
I have prayed for you that your faith will not fail.
(Luke 22:32)

At that moment I instantly recalled Cardinal Newman's motto: *Cor ad cor loquitur (Heart speaks to heart).* Be it by way of a fallen leaf or a chance verse, whether in the past we were "hugged or mugged, kicked or kissed," it is faith—sometimes clear, sometimes dark—that is our mainstay as we move on in years:

Now that I am old and my hair is gray,
do not abandon me, O God. (Psalm 71:18)

As a solitary leaf no longer contributes to the growth of the tree, senior friars may acutely realize that (and sometimes to their unjustified shame) that they are no longer "in the mainstream:"

Don't turn me out to pasture when I'm old
or put me on the shelf
when I can't pull my weight. (71:9, Peterson tr.)

There will come a time—maybe it has already made

its uninvited appearance–when the inevitable march of the years signals no turning back. The operetta *Babes in Toyland*, affirms the universal truth:

> *Toyland! Toyland! Little girl and boy land;*
> *Once you've crossed its borders*
> ***You can ne'er return again.***

Within every senior friar an interior voice, or at least a vague intuition, questions: "Now what? And what are my tasks, my new challenges?"

Faith with sister Hope whispers: "Adventure! Courage!"

> *Why be afraid that he may desert you, that he may toss you aside in your old age, when your strength has failed?* ***This is precisely the time when his strength will be in you, when your own is gone.*** (Augustine on Psalm 71)

With long cultivated Faith and Hope, the friar can calmly and surely embrace (at times with a heroism known only to himself) the opportunities of senior years:

> *A person is not old as long as they are seeking something. It's only when we sit back and let life go by that age sets in. What's your next dream in life? If you can't answer that question, get one."* (Jean Rostand)

Dreams can and will not only survive but flourish in the inevitable presence of hurdles that come with advancing years. To be sure. these are rightly perceived as losses which call for new ways, new paths:

To actively accept, with grace and minimum regret, one's past successes and failures...and go forward.

To recognize the feeling at times of being overlooked, unimportant or—worse—invisible...and embrace the lonely garden of Gethsemane.

To share the lessons and experiences of life but graciously allowing newer voices to be heard...and attended to with discernment.

To acknowledge, understandably with a tinge of sadness, that long-held ministerial and fraternal positions now require younger persons with creative perspectives...and respect what is fresh and innovative.

To recognize that driving a car has become dangerous... and a willingness to accept this enormous limitation to personal independence.

To accept that a truly loving community may no longer be able to provide physical and perhaps psychological care... and not see the assignment to a care center as an act of fraternal betrayal or indifference.

To draw encouragement and direction from another senior (Dag Hammarskjold)...

Forward! Thy orders are given in secret. May I always hear them—and obey.

Forward! Whatever distance I have covered, it does not give me the right to halt.

Forward! It is the attention given to the last steps before the summit which decides the value of all that went before.

WJR
August 2008